HISTORIC PHOTOS OF
HOBOKEN

TEXT AND CAPTIONS BY JOE CZACHOWSKI

TURNER
PUBLISHING COMPANY

Seen here on the Hudson in the late 1880s, the ferryboat *Hackensack* did not operate from its namesake New Jersey town but rather out of Hoboken. A number of the boats were named after towns such as Chautauqua, Passaic, and Hopatcong, whose names derived from Native American words.

HISTORIC PHOTOS OF
HOBOKEN

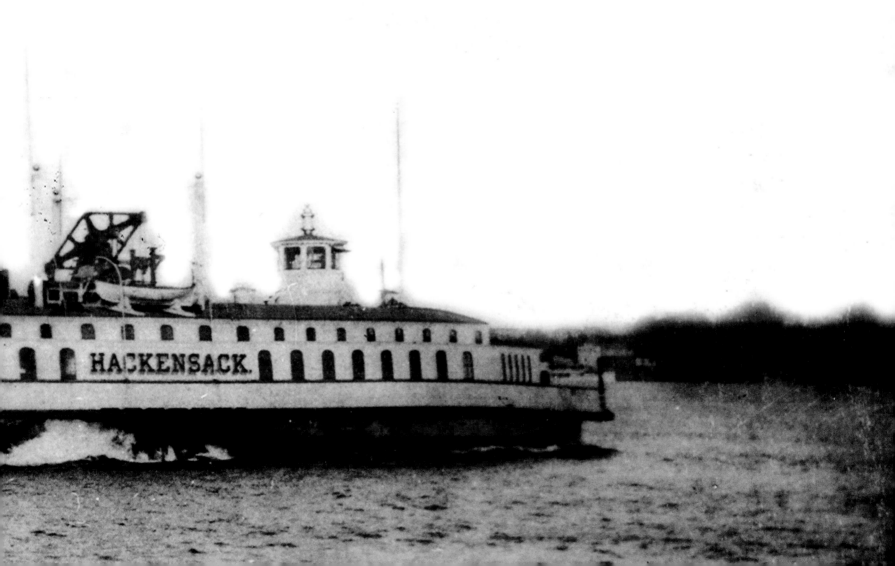

Turner Publishing Company
200 4th Avenue North • Suite 950
Nashville, Tennessee 37219
(615) 255-2665

www.turnerpublishing.com

Historic Photos of Hoboken

Library of Congress Control Number: 2008901712

ISBN-13:978-1-59652-443-9

Printed in the United States of America

08 09 10 11 12 13 14—0 9 8 7 6 5 4 3 2 1

CONTENTS

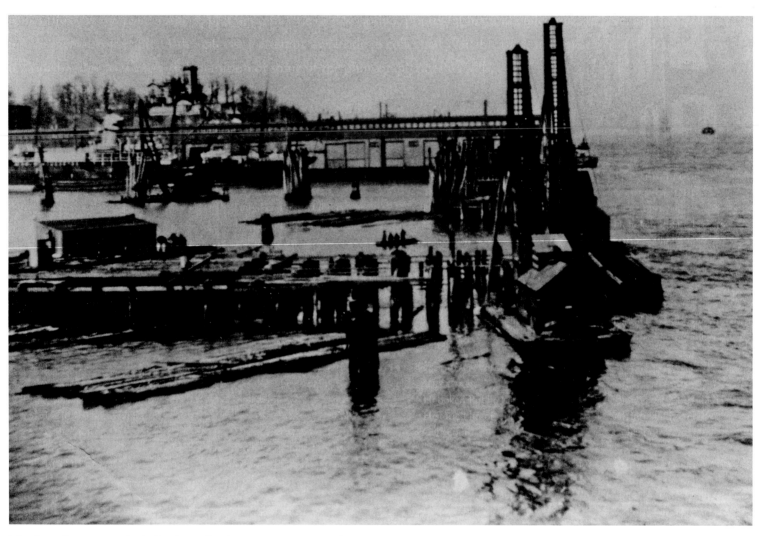

The first of many piers built for the Holland-America Line is seen here the way it appeared in the late 1880s. The pier was 600 feet long by 80 feet wide and was one story tall. It was the correct size for the time, but it would grow much larger soon enough.

ACKNOWLEDGMENTS

With the exception of cropping images where needed and touching up imperfections that have accrued over time, no other changes have been made to the photographs in this volume. The caliber and clarity of many photographs are limited by the technology of the day and the ability of the photographer at the time they were made.

This volume, *Historic Photos of Hoboken,* is the result of the cooperation and efforts of many individuals, organizations, and corporations. It is with great thanks that we acknowledge the valuable contribution of the following for their generous support:

Hoboken Public Library
New Jersey State Archives; Department of State

PREFACE

If you study New Jersey history, you will invariably encounter somewhere a statement along the lines of "New Jersey lives in the shadow of New York and Philadelphia." We roll with the punches here in Jersey, though, and have a few choice comments about that perception. However, when it comes to Hoboken specifically, the New Jersey port city did grow up in the shadow of a metropolis: New York. How Hoboken came into being, thrived, nearly died, and was revived, is a true American blue-collar success story.

In olden days Hoboken was a short boat ride from New York City, so in the bloom of spring, the wilting of summer, and the onset of autumn, New Yorkers would cross over the Hudson River and stroll along its western bank or through the Elysian Fields for a respite from the crowded city. Hoboken was a part of the natural harbor, so it was only a matter of time before it became an integral part of the economic system of the entire area. The city's growth brought immigrants looking for work, which they found first in the shipping business then in manufacturing and transportation. Hoboken became a hardworking, tough, immigrant city, a draw for the Italian, German, Dutch, Irish, and Eastern European masses who yearned for that breath of fresh air on America's golden shores.

Hoboken can claim its fair share of firsts. In 1663 America's first brewery was patented at Castle Point. With all apologies to Cooperstown, New York, Hoboken hosted the first organized baseball game, on June 19, 1846. The first zipper was manufactured by Hoboken's Automatic Hook & Eye Company. Thomas Edison drove the first electrified train from Hoboken's Delaware, Lackawanna, & Western Terminal to Montclair, New Jersey. Colonel John Stevens, whose family was responsible for establishing most of the town and also Stevens Institute of Technology, ran the first steam-powered ferry and implemented technical changes that enabled steam locomotives to be adapted from the English version to the American type that eventually spanned the continent. His son Robert Stevens designed the "T-rail" track still used in railroad engineering today. The Blimpie brand of fast-food sandwich was first served on Hoboken's Washington Street.

A Hoboken location served as inspiration for Edgar Allen Poe's eerie tale "The Mystery of Marie Roget." The city's name has been used in entertainment settings from Looney Toons cartoons to a *Twilight Zone* episode. Hoboken's famous residents have included the artist Willem de Kooning, the actress and *Titanic* survivor Dorothy Gibson, the sex researcher Alfred Kinsey, the alternative rock band the Bongos, and that somewhat successful singer Francis Albert Sinatra.

With success comes eventual downturn. Hoboken's rise was high and fairly consistent for a number of decades, but its demise was swift. In the mid-1950s the city was used as a backdrop for the Academy Award–winning film *On the Waterfront*. The black-and-white film with its stark contrasts seemed to cast a pall over the real city. The shipyards began to close and were gone by the late 1960s. Manufacturing was relocated, and the city became depressed economically as well as socially and spiritually. The heart of the city became chilled. The sun continued to rise, however, and someone remembered what Hoboken was in the first place: a welcome respite from the city.

As business boomed in New York City, Hoboken's land value increased. Old factories and abandoned warehouses were either removed or converted to apartments and condominiums. A new wave of transplants came to Hoboken and brought it back to its former identity as a vibrant city of people, culture, and history. As I sat in a park across from the Hoboken Public Library, the air was filled with other tongues—Spanish, Italian, German—along with English, and with the laughter and delightful squeals of children playing; this is the same in any language. With the fall of the World Trade Center, just across a short span of the harbor, the city once again felt a great loss, yet it managed to overcome this tragedy to rebound and be in the sunlight once again.

—Joe Czachowski

Fischer's Boots & Shoes was located on 1st Street, as seen in this view looking west.

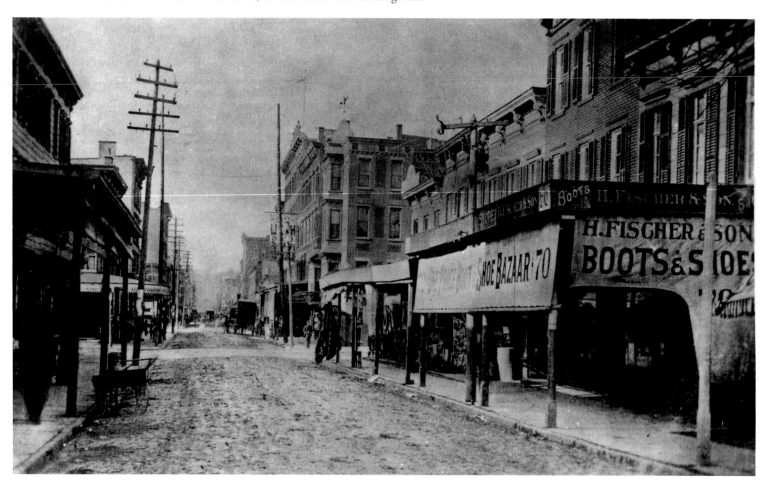

HOBOKEN LAND AND IMPROVEMENT

(1860–1899)

Hoboken is a two-square-mile plot of land along the Hudson River. Of this, one and one-half miles is waterfront, and while "dirt is gold" in real estate, the city also possesses a harbor channel that is 60 feet deep.

Hoboken was first sighted by Henry Hudson from on board his *Half Moon* in 1609. The origin of the name Hoboken is in dispute as deriving from either the Lenape Indian *Hopoghan* or the Dutch/Flemish *Hooge Buechen,* or an actual Van Hoboken family from the Netherlands. The Old Dutch term *Hoebuck,* or "high bluff," might be the proper fit. The town land was passed from Michael Pauw to Teunissen Van Patten to Samuel Bayard, who remained loyal to the English during the American Revolution. So after the war the newly confiscated land was purchased by Colonel John Stevens, who kept a parcel for his family and donated the rest to become Hoboken, the town his family would dominate for over 100 years.

Stevens developed the land as a resort for New Yorkers looking for a leisurely stroll on a fair day. He instituted the first steam ferry in 1811. The attraction Sybil's Cave opened in 1832, bringing guests to its spring waters and inspiring Edgar Allen Poe to write a mystery. Stevens then founded the Hoboken Land and Improvement Company; he and his family used the company to map out the city and develop its many uses, which included the waterfront. In 1870 the family established the Stevens Institute of Technology, one of the foremost technical schools in the nation, producing at least two Nobel Prize winners.

Hoboken's favorable location was not lost on potential developers of shipping interests. Terminals were built for many steamship lines, including North German Lloyd and Hamburg-American. This led to the presence of a large German population in the city in its early years. Dry docks were also built for construction and repair.

The growth of Hoboken was steady and rapid for a variety of reasons. Easy access from Europe was the main cause, not just from Germany but from all countries expunging their "wretched refuse." Commercial growth expanded as well, and banking institutions were quickly established. The city was incorporated March 28, 1855, but it had been well on its way years before that official act.

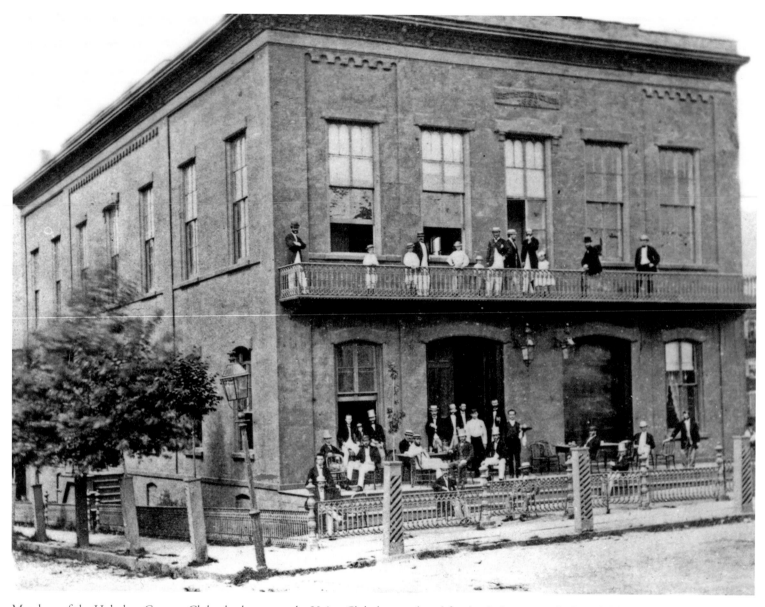

Members of the Hoboken German Club, also known as the Union Club, have gathered for the day's events, which probably included posing for this mid-1860s photograph. The club was organized in 1857, and the building was located at the northwest corner of 6th and Hudson streets.

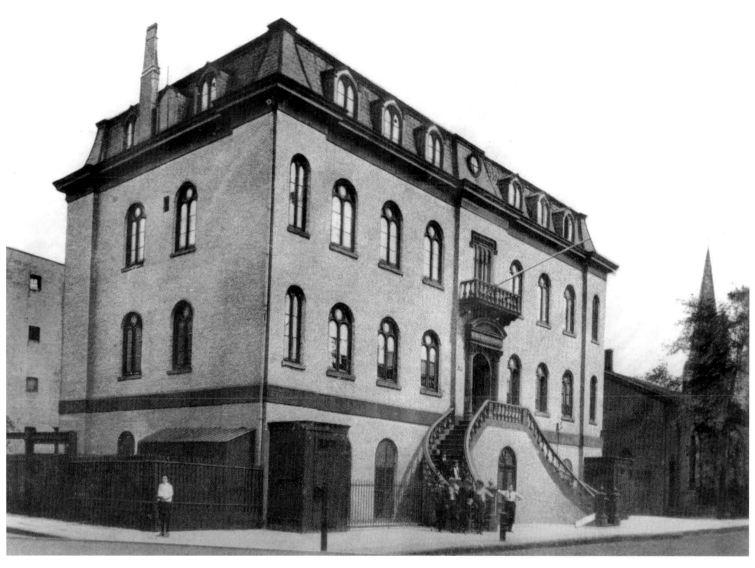

The Martha Institute at 6th Street and Park Avenue was established in the 1860s as an industrial-arts training school for boys. It later housed the Stanley Society, named for the well-known explorer Henry Morton Stanley and dedicated to the study of Africa.

During the Civil War, Captain William Hexamer, at left, commanded 151 Hoboken volunteers in Battery A of the 1st New Jersey Artillery. The Hoboken unit served in 40 major engagements and has monuments dedicated to it on the battlefields of Gettysburg and Antietam. Captain Hexamer died in Hoboken in 1870.

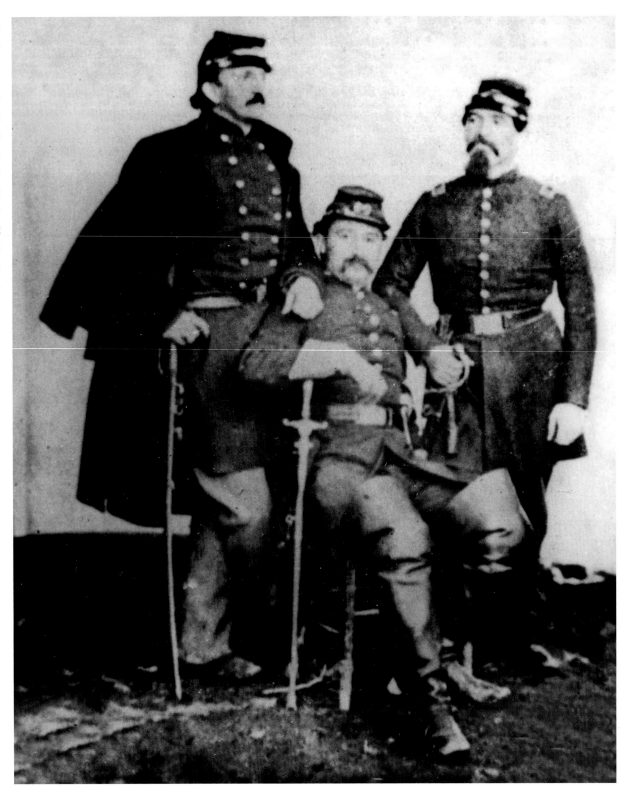

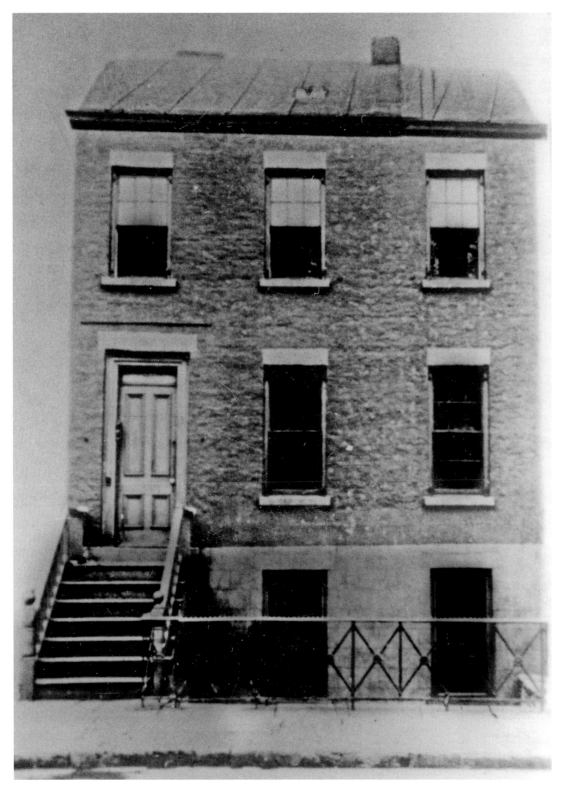

St. Mary's Hospital was founded in this building in 1863. It is hard to overstate the importance to Hoboken of this hospital, which grew with the community. As a Catholic hospital, its mission included care for the poor. It served as an embarkation hospital before World War I and as a convalescent hospital after, and it was a haven during the influenza epidemic of 1918.

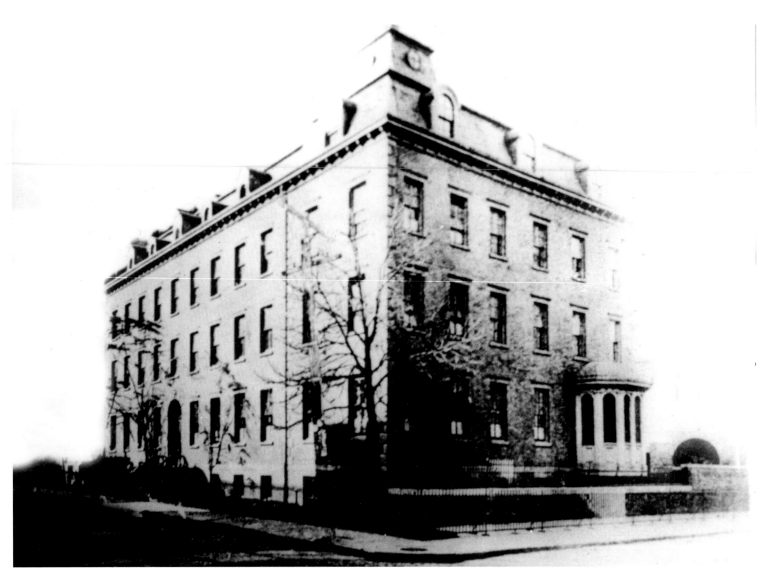

By 1866, three years after its founding, St. Mary's Hospital had already been enlarged. It would become as important to the people of Hoboken as any house of worship or civic entity, and it had begun to serve a growing immigrant population in addition to the town's native-born residents.

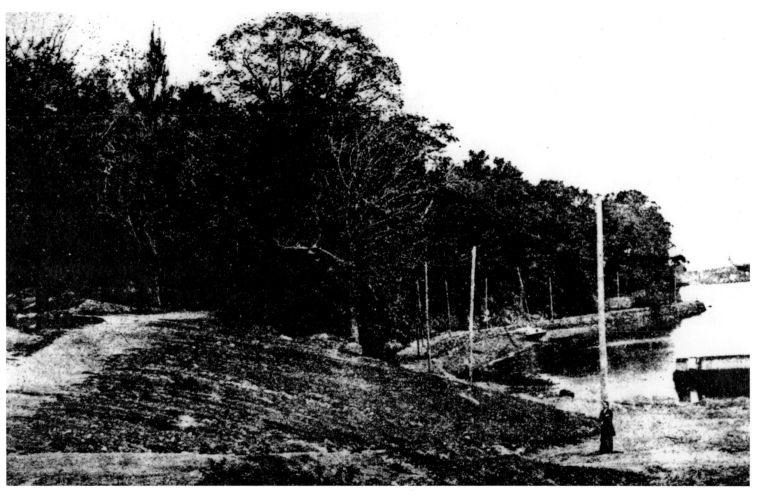

A person can be seen standing alone in this 1865 view north from the foot of 5th Street. Could that person have possibly imagined how this pastoral setting would be transformed in the years to come into a bustling port and manufacturing city?

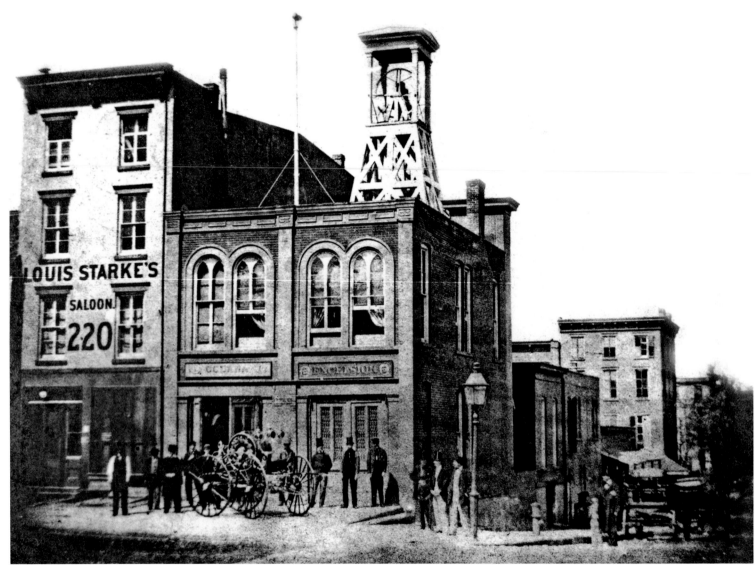

This firehouse seen in 1868 at the southwest corner of Washington and 6th streets probably housed Oceana Company No. 1 and Excelsior No. 2. Note the bell tower on the roof and Starke's Saloon next door. Men in front are inspecting one of the fire wagons.

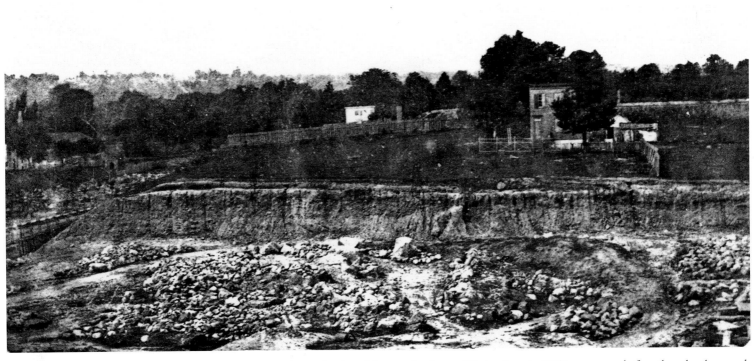

This view shows the site of Stevens Institute of Technology in 1868, two years before the school opened.

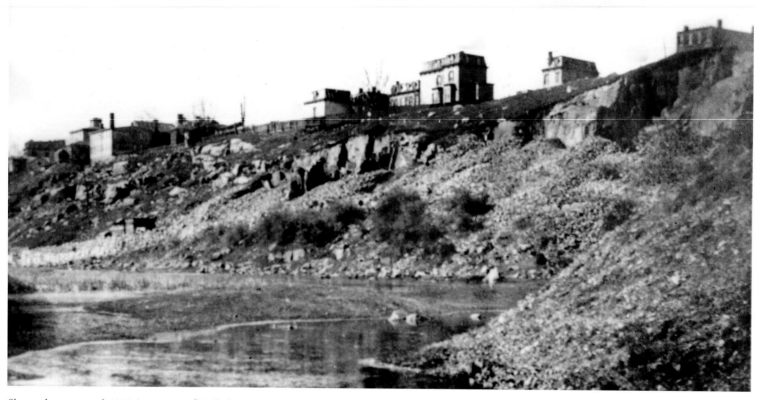

Shown here around 1870 is an area of Hoboken near where the Delaware, Lackawanna, and Western Railroad (DL&WRR) tunnel beneath the Hudson River would be completed. Samuel Rockwell, resident engineer of the DL&WRR, was responsible for the project.

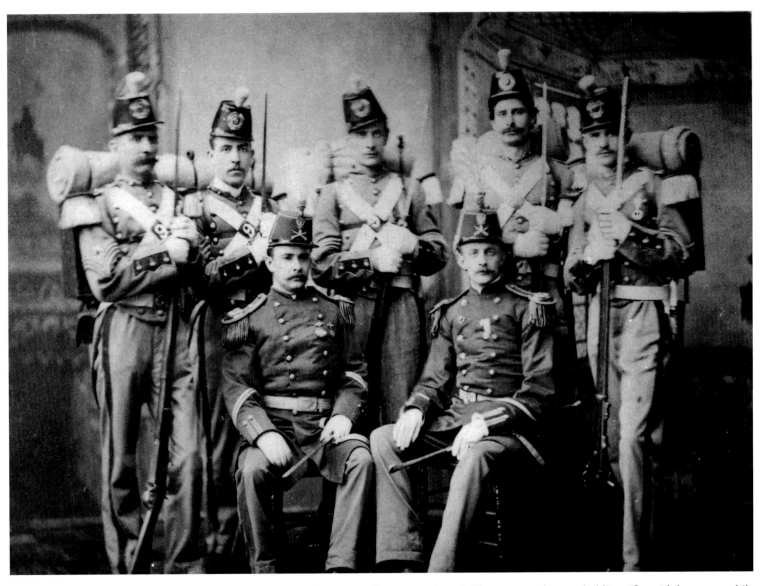

Hoboken war veterans in full uniform pose for a group photo around 1875. The men standing are holding rifles with bayonets, while the seated officers have riding crops.

This Hoboken Fire Department bell tower on Park Avenue near 2nd Street, seen around the late 1870s, stood among the area's tenement buildings so all residents would have access in case of conflagration. The large pipes on the ground may indicate construction in the growing city.

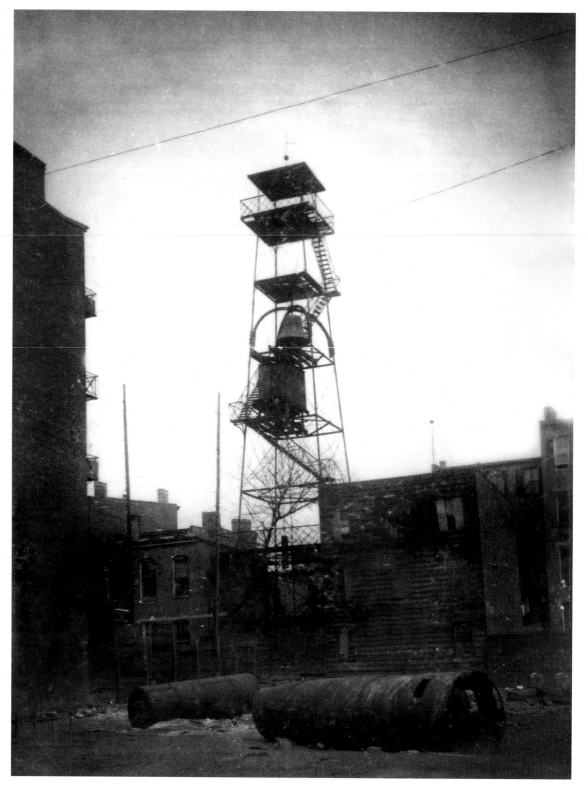

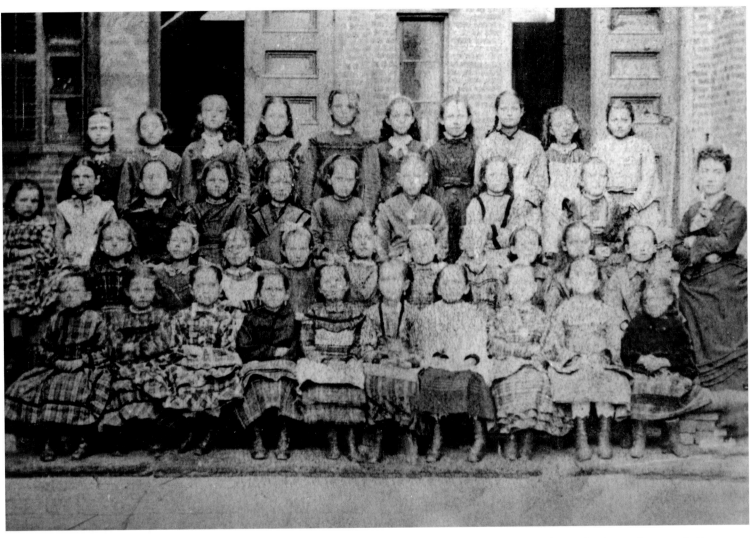

This is the 1870 class photo of Hoboken's No. 2 School on Garden between 9th and 10th streets. It appears that at the time only young ladies were enrolled.

The Independent Order of Odd Fellows was established in England to give aid to those in need and to pursue projects for public good. The Hoboken Odd Fellows Hall, seen here around the 1870s, was located on Washington between 4th and 5th streets.

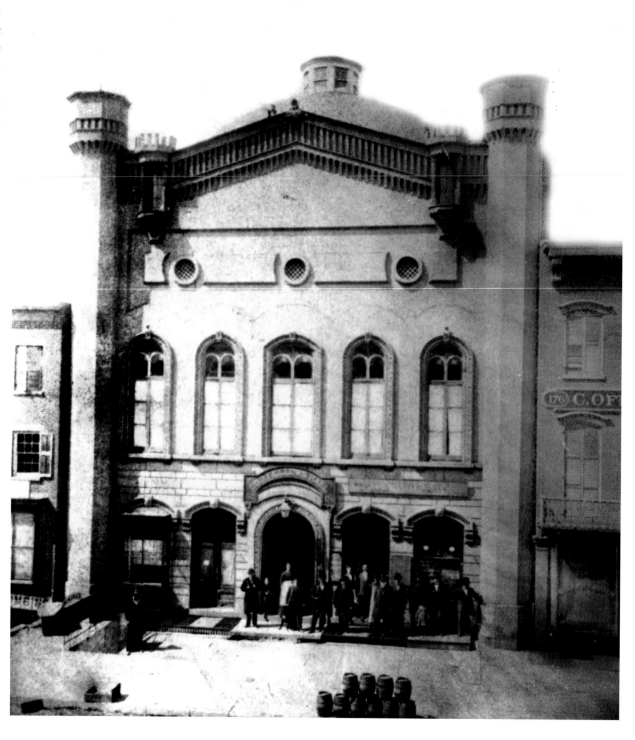

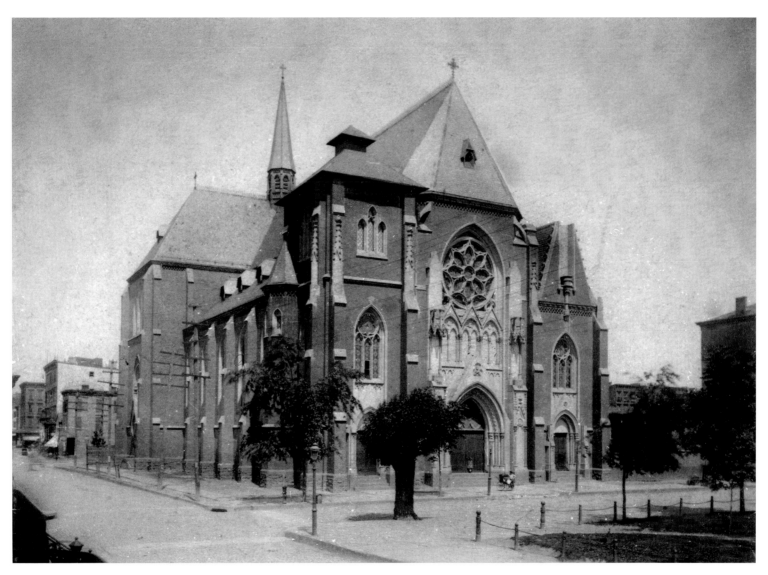

Our Lady of Grace Church was built in 1878 at 4th Street and Willow Avenue and is seen here shortly after its completion. Designed in the German Gothic style by Hoboken resident Francis George Hempler, it serves one of the oldest Catholic parishes in the United States. In its time it was the largest church in New Jersey, and it is now on the National Register of Historic Places.

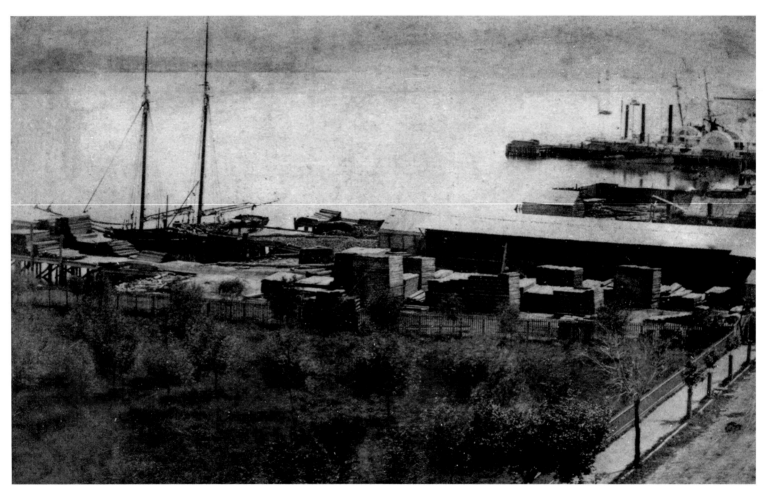

This southward view of a pier on River Street shows the harbor area beginning to take shape in the 1880s, with a few docks and ships and a lumber yard visible. The lumber was only construction material, but wood and sparks don't mix well, especially off the water. When boilers were put on the boats and ships, danger beckoned.

Stevens Institute dominates this 1870s view from River between 3rd and 4th streets.

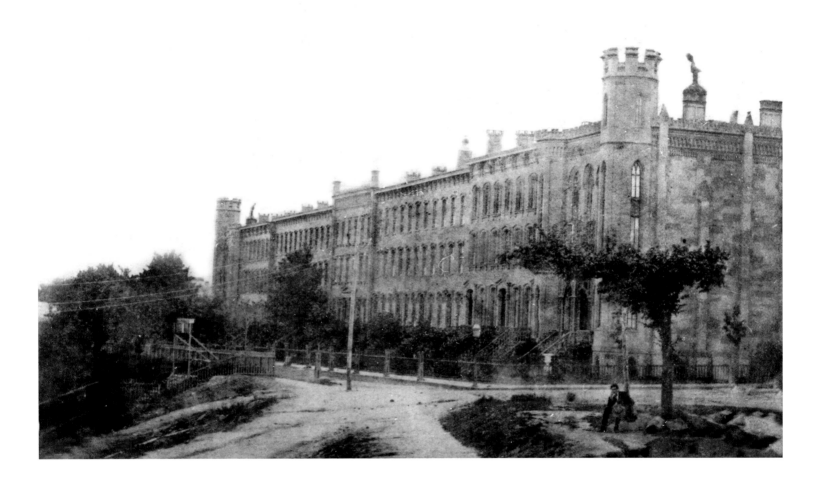

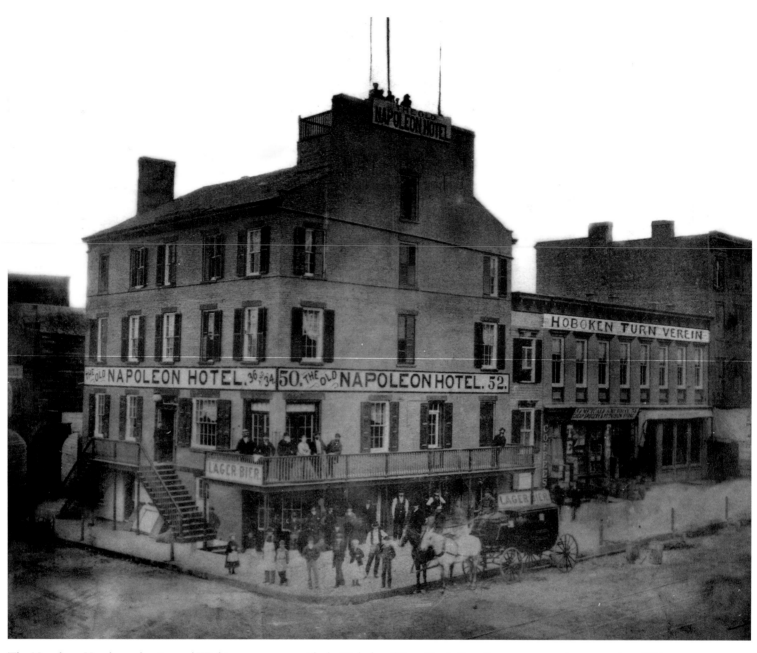

The Napoleon Hotel stood at 1st and Washington streets, with the Hoboken "Turn Verein," or German gymnasium, next door. This 1871 scene illustrates that photography was still a novelty, as everyone seems to be facing the camera. People are even on the roof.

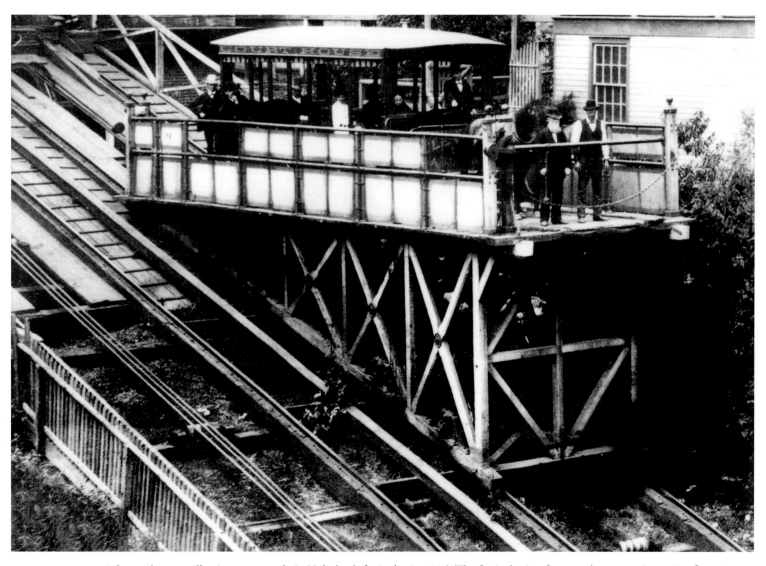

A horse-drawn trolley is transported via Hoboken's funicular in 1874. The funicular is a fourteenth-century invention for going up an incline too steep for conventional rails. In the conventional system the steel wheels on steel track would not be able to maintain traction, so in the funicular system a cable pulls one car up while another car going the opposite way provides balance.

Trolley tracks can be seen in front of the 2nd Precinct Police Station at Willow Avenue and 12th Street.

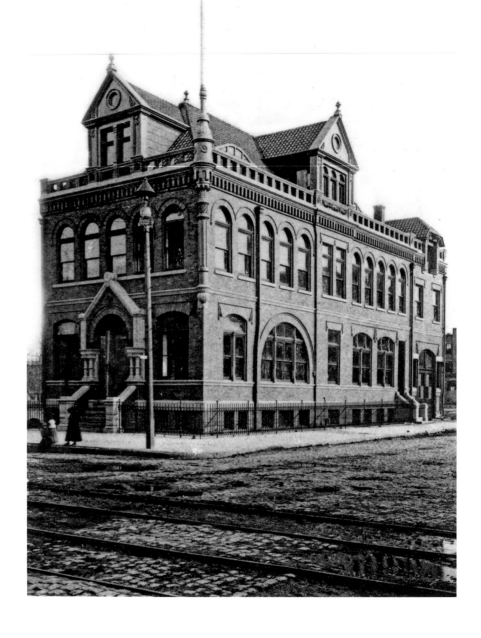

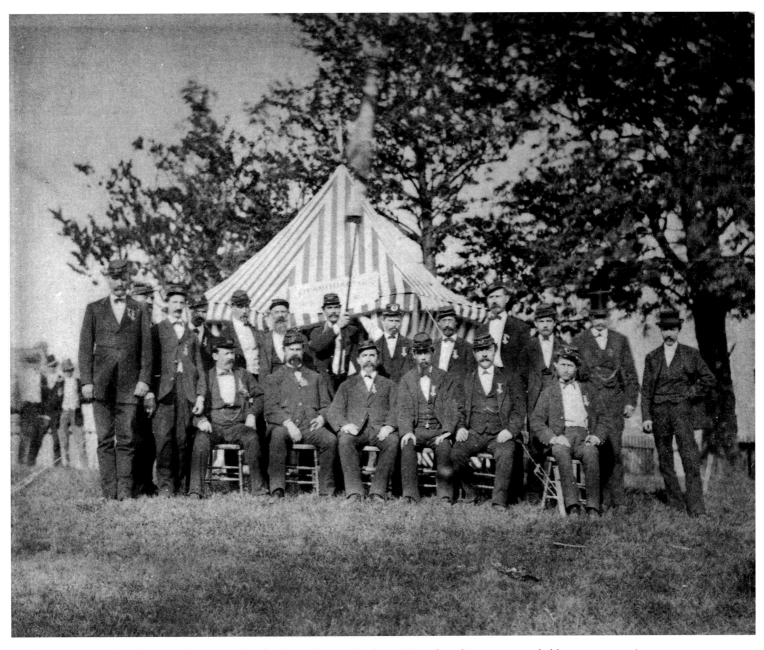

Civil War veterans of Hoboken gather in 1875 at the Otto Cottage Garden at Newark and 1st streets, probably commemorating a decade of peace.

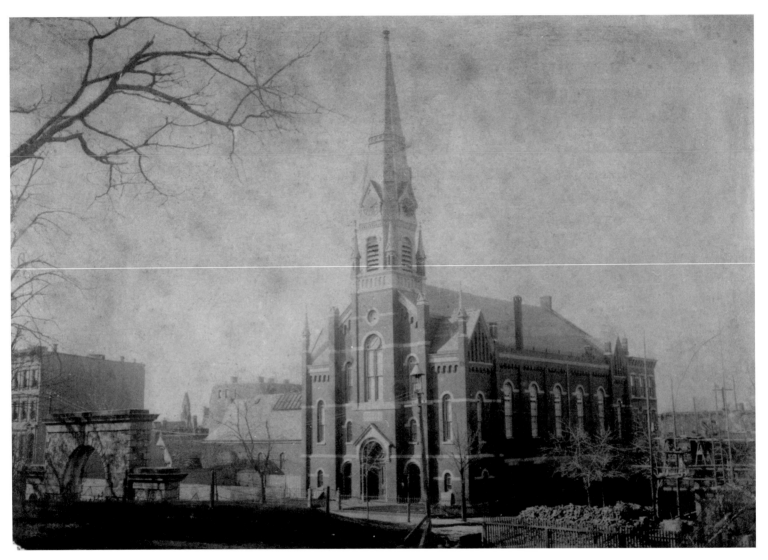

One of the longest-established congregations in the city of Hoboken is that of St. Matthew's German Evangelical Lutheran Church at the corner of 8th and Hudson streets, seen here in the 1880s. Organized in 1858, the congregation occupied a former Presbyterian church before the current structure was completed. The towering steeple with its bell and clock rises to a height of 150 feet. The first pastor was Reverend C. M. Wassiddlo.

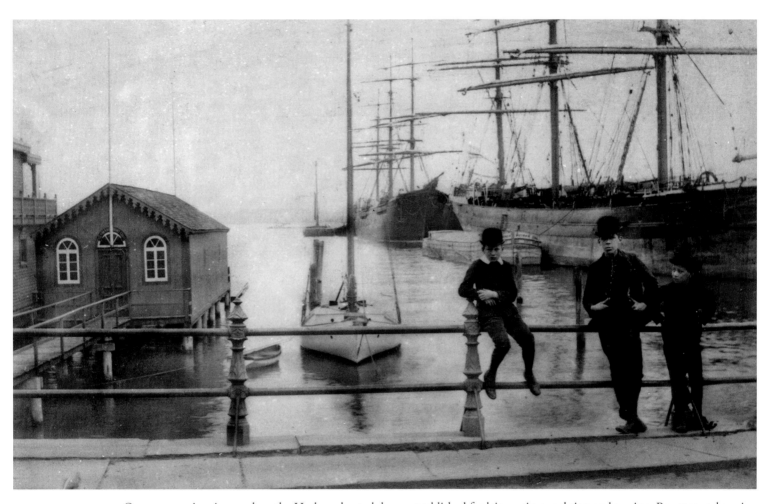

On an expansive river such as the Hudson, boat clubs are established for leisure-time yachting and rowing. Regattas and rowing meets become social events and tests of strength and skill, and heated rivalries develop. Here is the Germania Boat Club, located at the foot of 4th Street, in the 1880s. The mixture of commerce and pleasure is evident. Perhaps the three lads are waiting for the tide to turn.

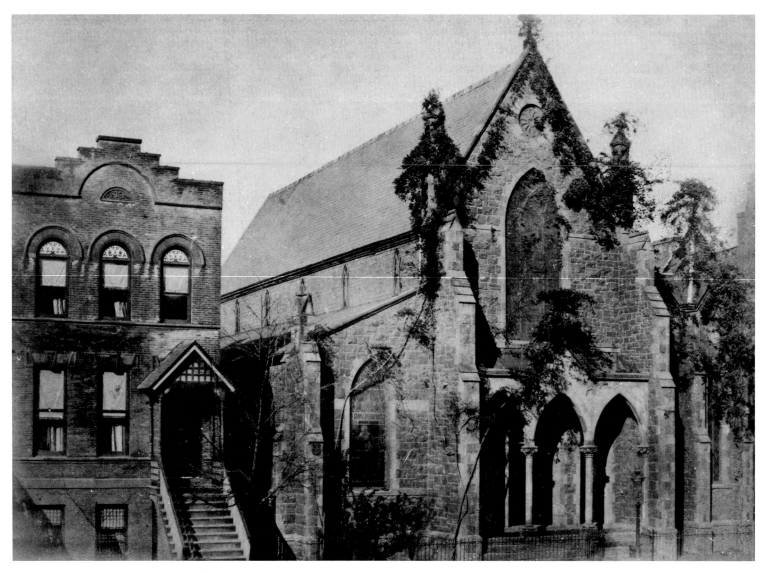

The congregation represented by St. Paul's Episcopal Church held its first service in Hoboken in 1832. This St. Paul's building, seen in the 1880s, was on Hudson Street between 8th and 9th streets. The first rector was Reverend John A. Wood.

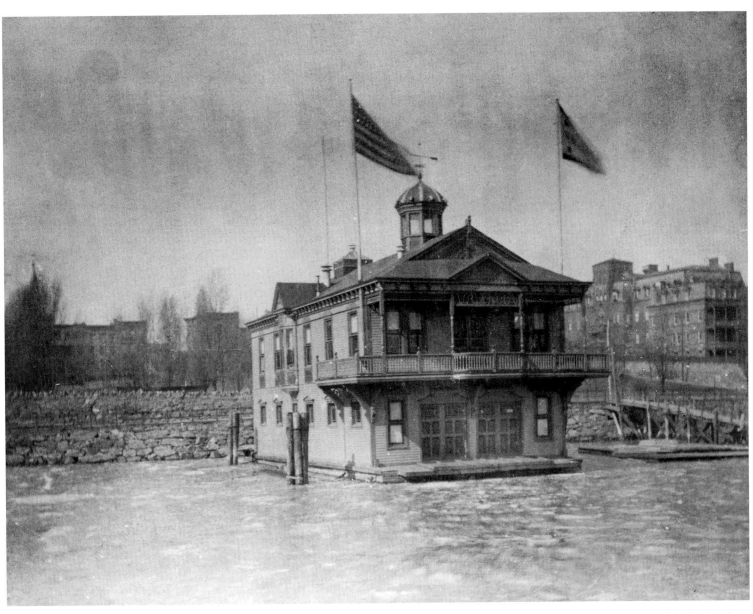

The Valencia Boat Club seen here around 1880 was located at the foot of 5th Street. Organized in 1874, it was one of the leading boat clubs along the Hoboken section of the Hudson River, and the club structure was considered one of the most handsome on either bank. The 100-member club had a reputation for social activities, as represented by a riding club, an orchestra, and a bowling team.

The Odd Fellows Hall, seen here around 1890, seems to have literally had its roof raised at some point in the preceding decade, with another floor added. The change is indicative of the growth in many aspects of Hoboken life.

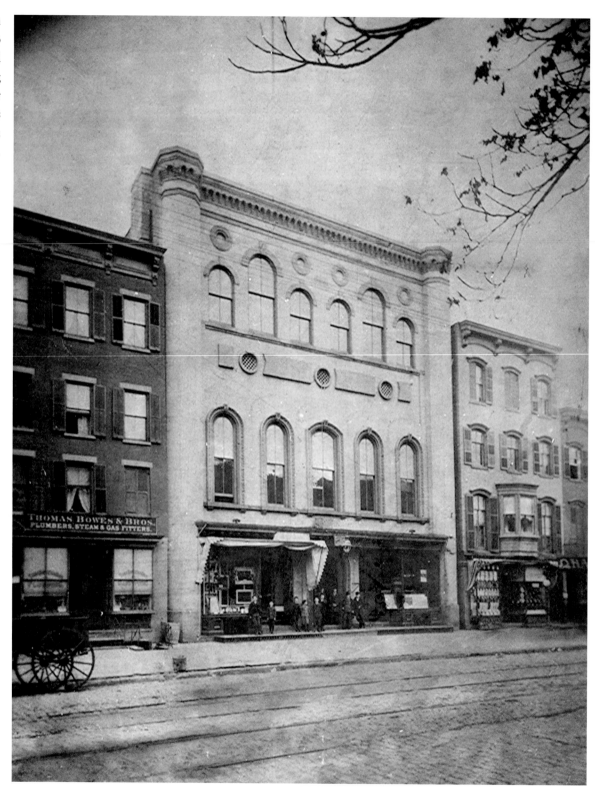

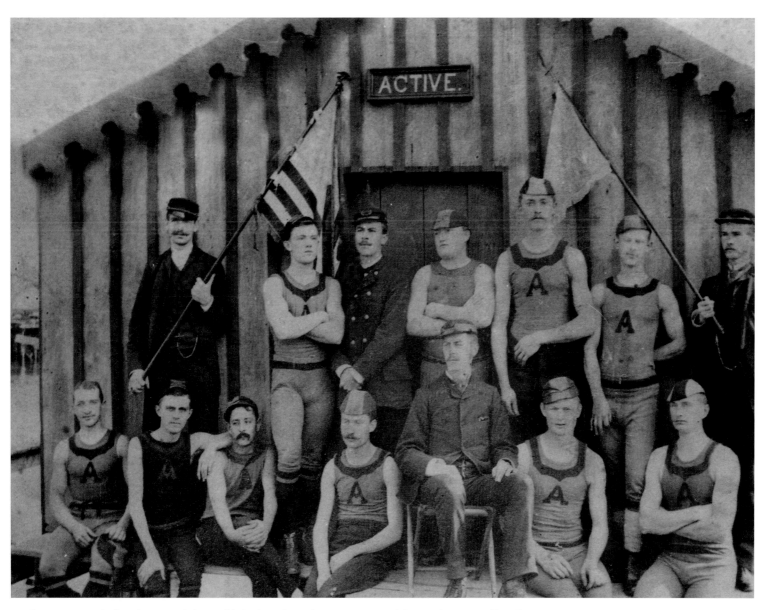

With so many Hoboken boating clubs established, such as the Active Boat Club seen here, as well as those in nearby New York, matches were always in vogue if the river wasn't frozen.

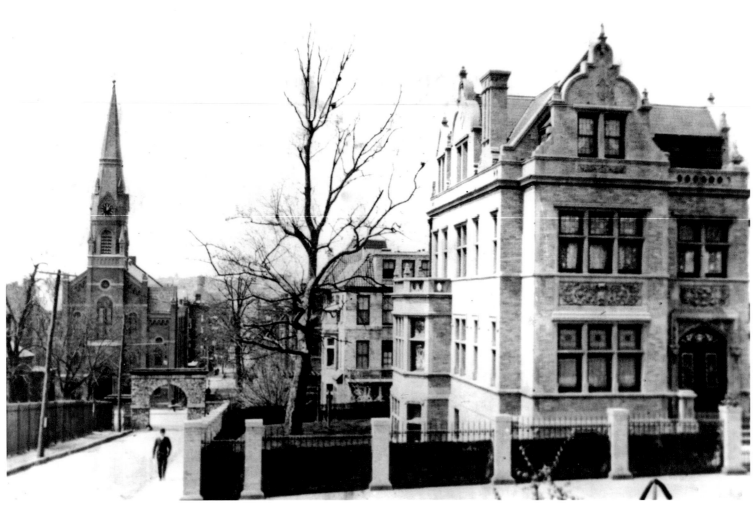

An elegant home built for the Behren family graces the corner of Castle Point Terrace and 8th Street, with St. Matthew's German Lutheran Church in the background.

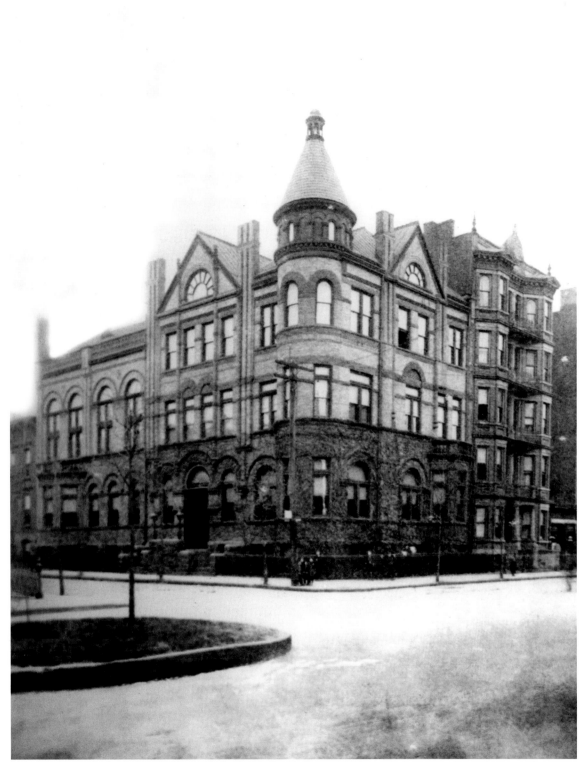

The Columbia Club, a "gentleman's society" of 100 men from Hoboken and New York City, was located at 11th and Bloomfield streets in Hoboken. This 1890s view shows the elegant style of architect Henry Hobson Richardson; the rounded archways and tower bespeak Richardson's interest in Romanesque style. The building was later the home of Euclid Masonic Lodge #35.

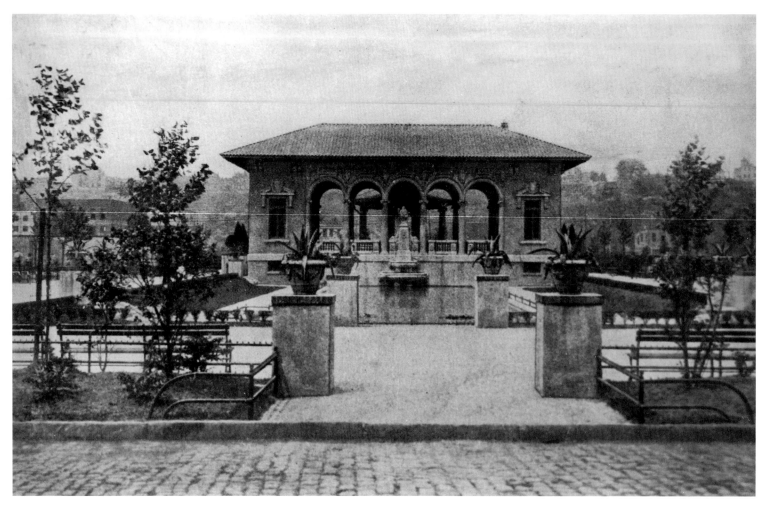

Columbus Park offered one of the first athletic fields in Hoboken, a city by then cramped for open space. This 1880s image shows a grand structure inviting visitors to escape from the city's crowded conditions.

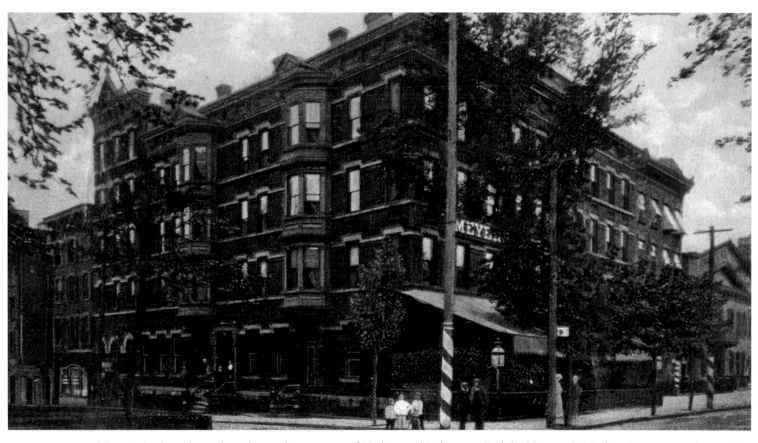

Meyers Hotel was located on the southeast corner of Hudson and 3rd streets. Built by Herman L. Timken, it was a popular meeting spot for community organizations and political clubs of all persuasions. Here the utility poles are adorned like candy canes for a festive occasion.

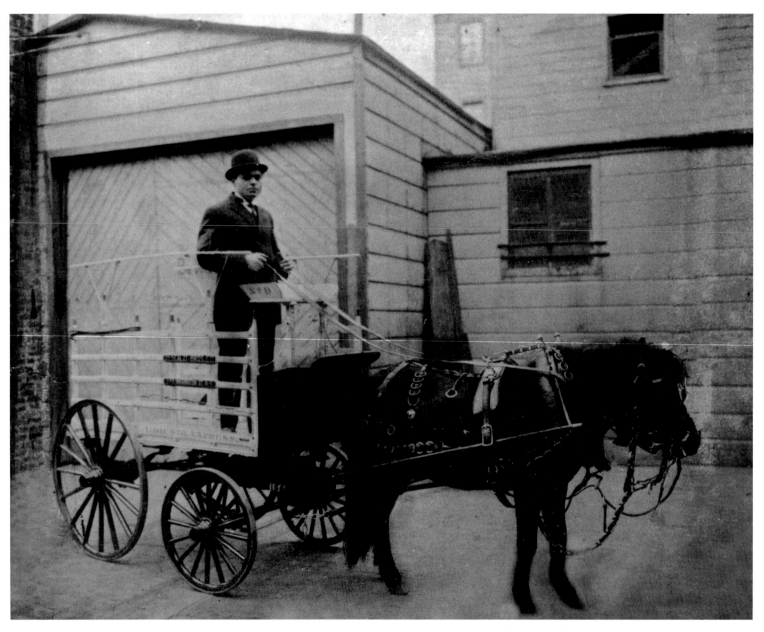

If you want to be a teamster you have to start somewhere, and Hoboken was a place where you could start small and dream big. Here the founder of the Gusto Trucking Company holds the reins, probably during the 1870s.

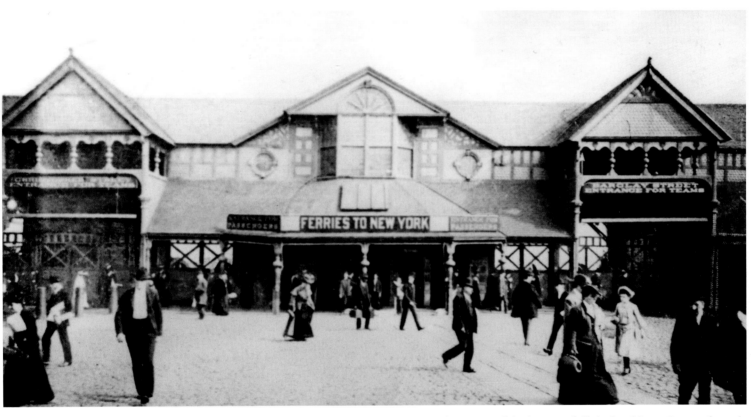

The ferry from Barclay Street in Hoboken to Christopher Street in New York was one of the busiest of all the local lines. Scores of people availed themselves of its use both for themselves and for their horse-drawn wagons, as attested to by the "entrance for teams" sign.

Seen here in the 1880s, the Colonnade House, known later as McCarty's Hotel, apparently was a popular spot for people to gather after baseball games and other sporting events played on the nearby Elysian Fields. There are numerous accounts of games being "replayed" into the wee hours of the morning over large glasses of lager.

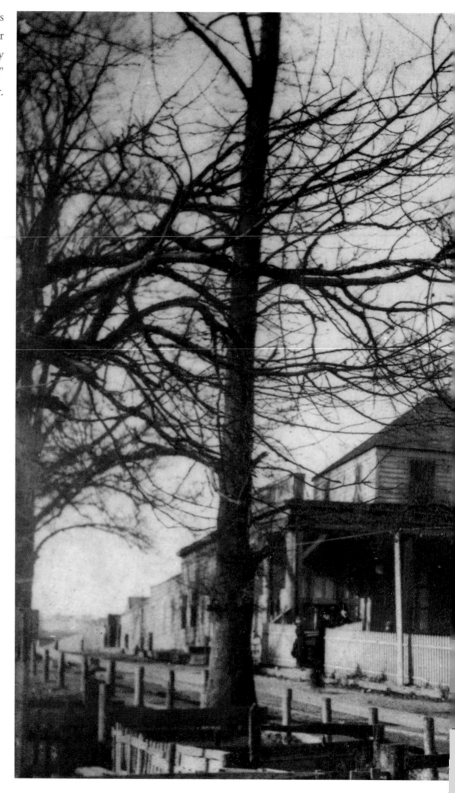

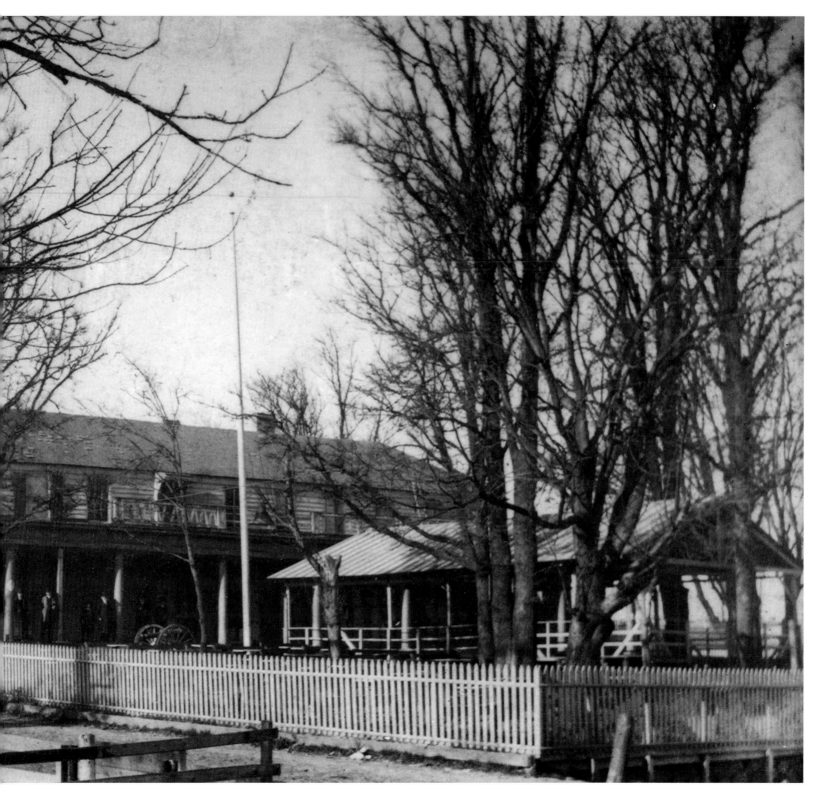

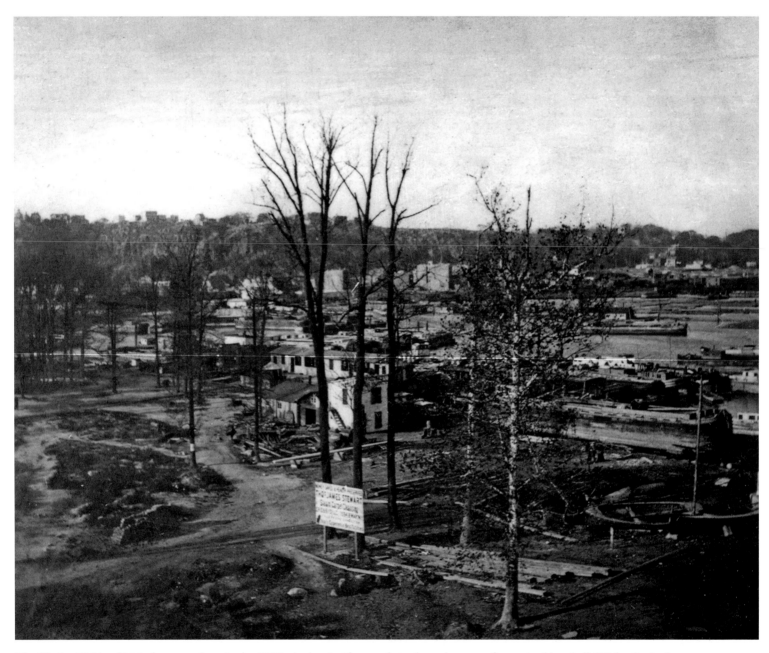

The Elysian Fields of Hoboken, seen here in the 1880s, had a significant role in the early years of organized baseball. With a limited amount of space in New York City, teams would often go to Hoboken to play. The first organized game was played at the Elysian Fields on June 19, 1846, between Alexander Cartwright's Knickerbockers and the New York Nine. Journalist Harry Chadwick promoted the use of the fields and became instrumental in the development of the national pastime.

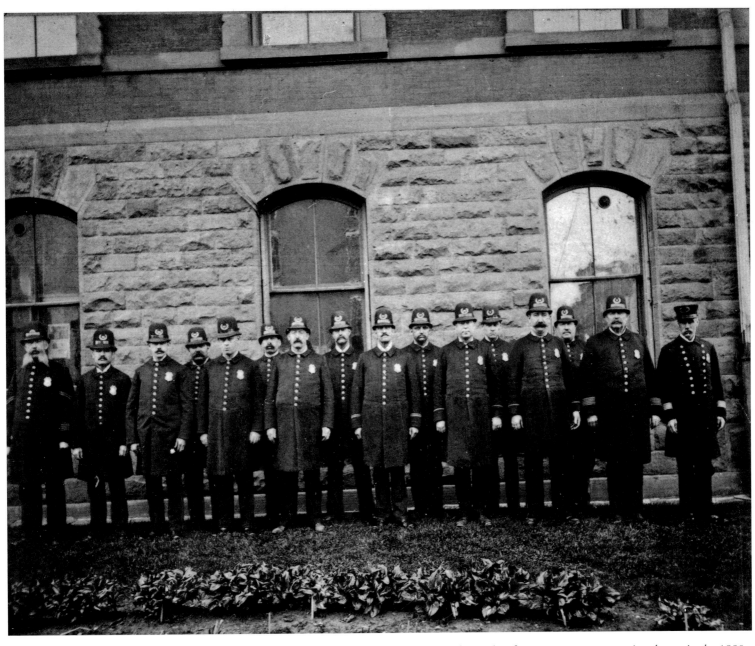

Members of the Hoboken police force pose next to a precinct house in the 1880s.

A horse-drawn trolley saunters down Willow Avenue near 11th Street. The aptly named Willow Avenue Line announced itself with signage on the side of the car.

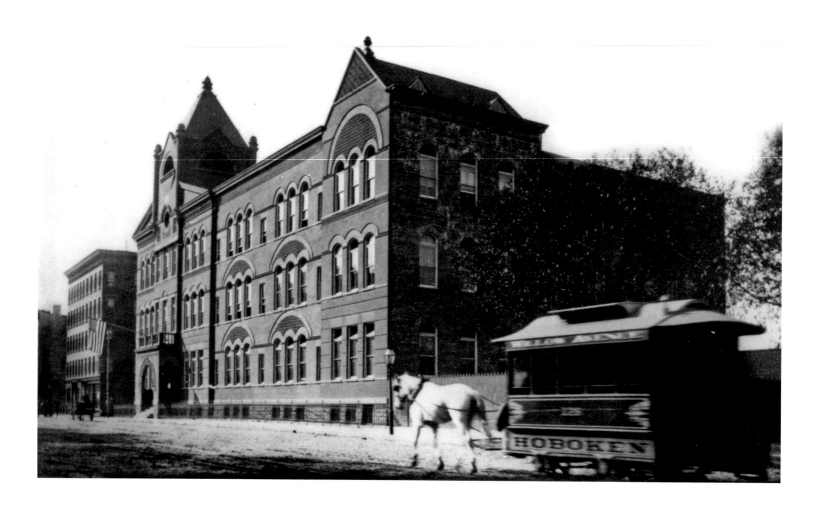

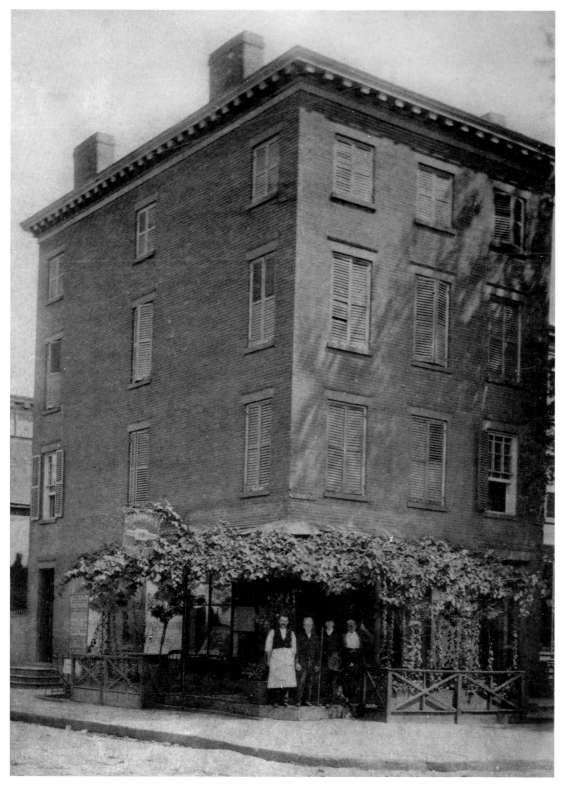

On the corner of Newark and Washington streets stood Michael Coyle's Liquors and Tavern, seen here in the 1890s with the bartender and three others out front. Coyle was active in local politics, a good melding of business and pleasure. The Fabian Theatre later occupied this corner.

This large home with the expansive lawn on both sides was located on Hudson Street near 10th Street. Seen here in the 1880s, it was owned at different times by the Reiche family, the Crusius family, and later Lawrence Fagan, a Hoboken mayor and owner of the Fagan Ironworks that burned in 1905.

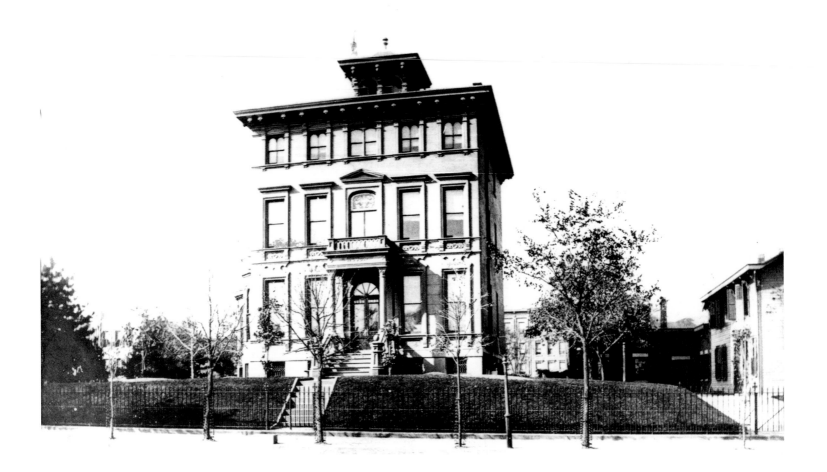

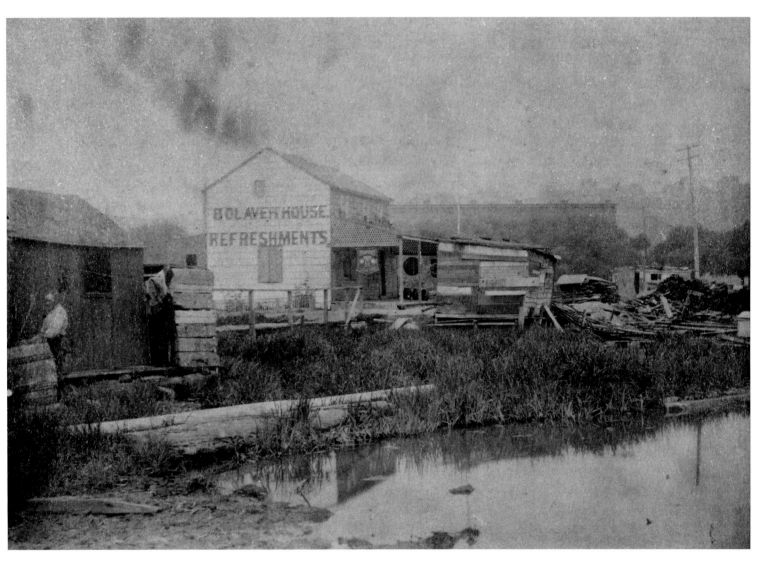

The Bolaver House at 11th Street and Park Avenue served refreshments to the workers in the area during the 1880s and 1890s.

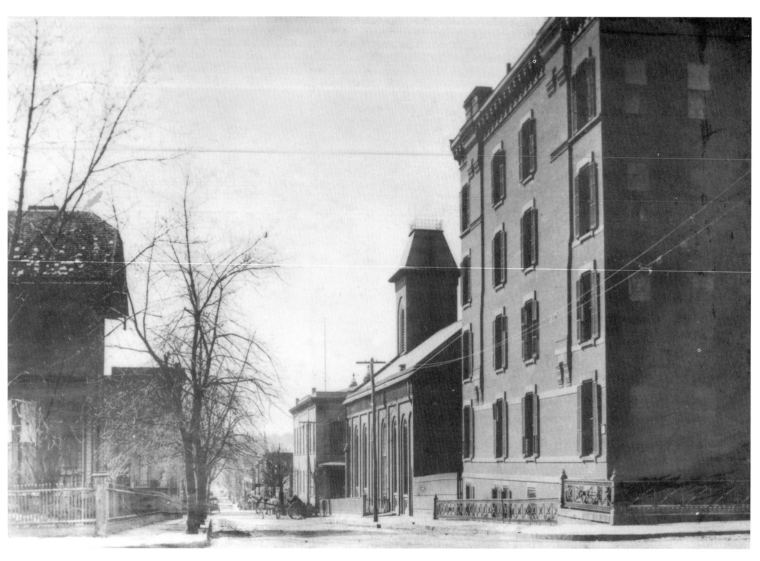

This 1880s view west from River and 6th streets includes the First Presbyterian Church located at 6th and Hudson.

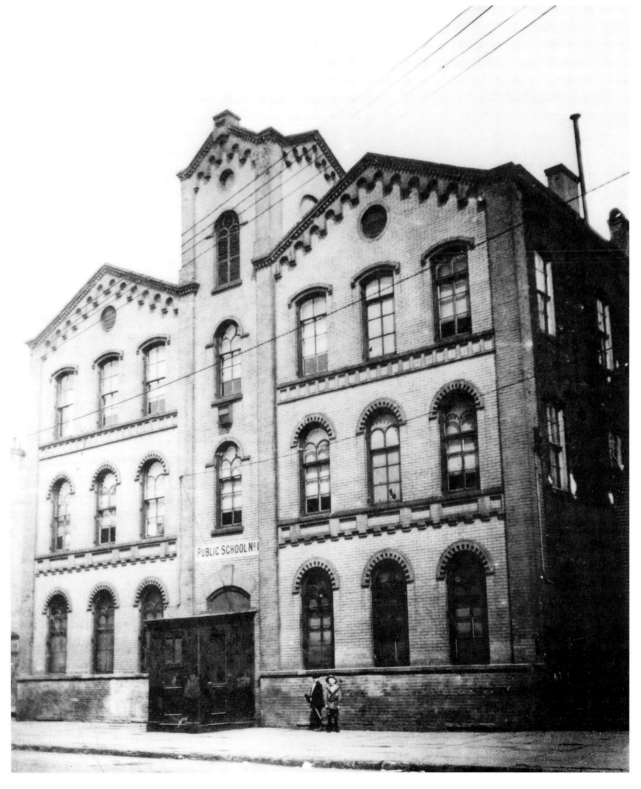

Seen here in the latter years of the nineteenth century, Hoboken's Public School No. 1 was located on Garden Street near 3rd Street.

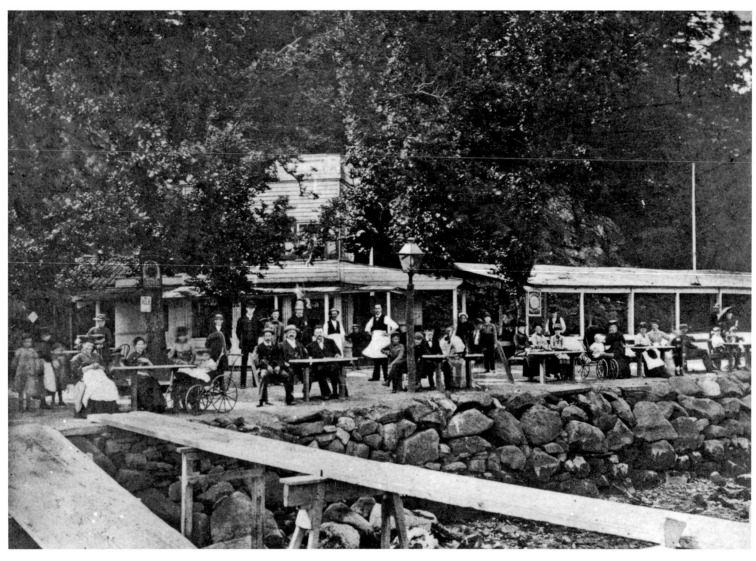

This 1890s view from a not too sturdy-looking walkway out toward the Hudson shows a leisurely scene near Sybil's Cave, a local attraction. Sightseers and tavern customers are enjoying themselves. Note the large-wheeled baby strollers.

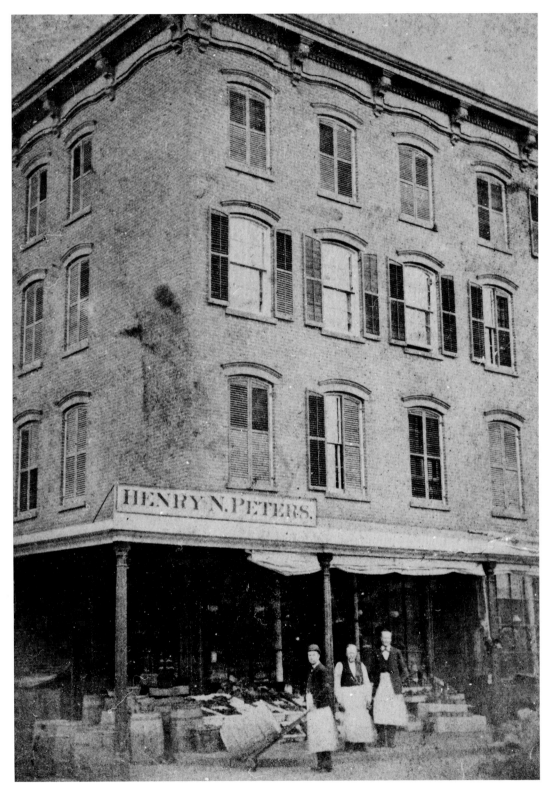

Henry Peters owned a grocery store at 223 Washington Street on the corner with 6th Street. In this 1880s scene, barrels are being moved by the staff. Perhaps a shipment of goods had just arrived in port from somewhere overseas.

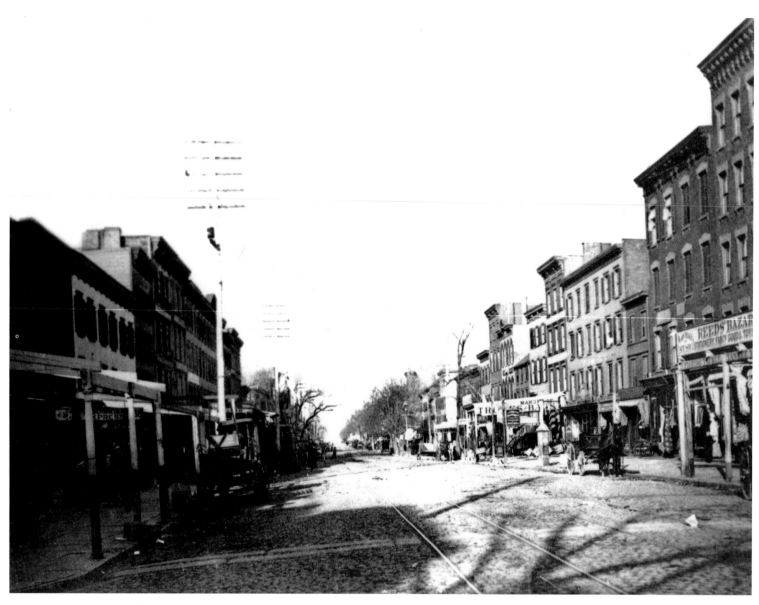

On the sunny side of Washington Street in 1885, an apparent calm prevails before the shoppers arrive.

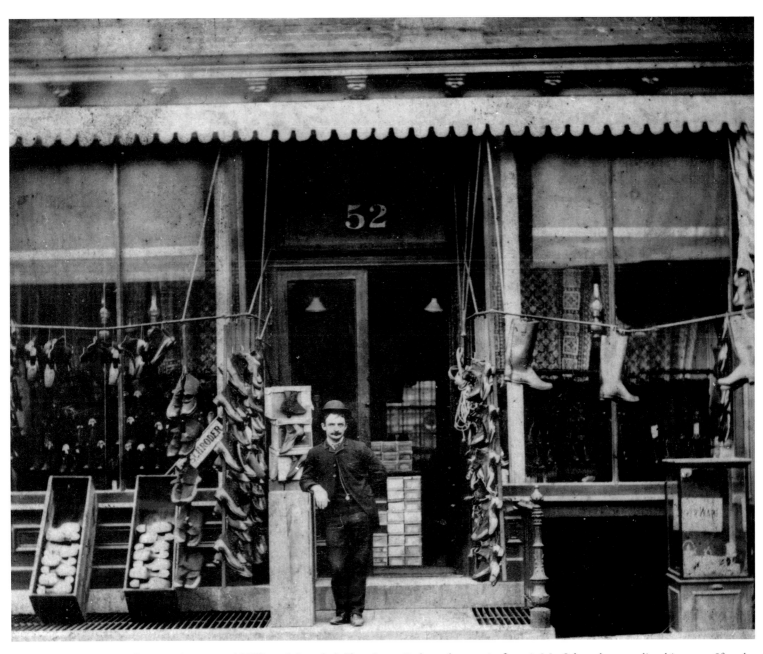

At 52 Washington Street stood William Schroeder's Shoe Store. Perhaps the man in front is Mr. Schroeder, guarding his wares. If so, he would have hoped to soon have customers shrinking his large inventory of boots and shoes of all kinds and sizes.

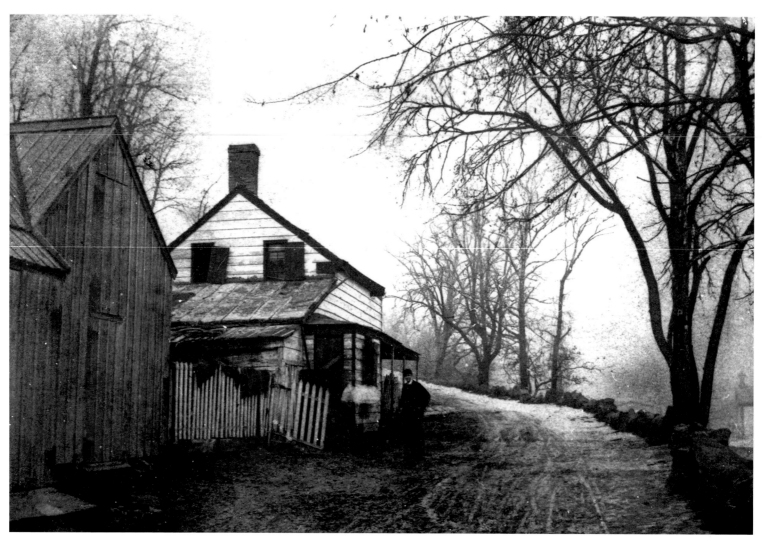

Above the intersection of Willow Avenue and 19th Street stood the Hoboken Toll Gate, which was the end of the Old Hackensack Plank Road. A plank road is as it sounds, a dirt road or path covered with wooden planks to allow easier travel. The toll gate house appears to be run down; perhaps time to raise the toll.

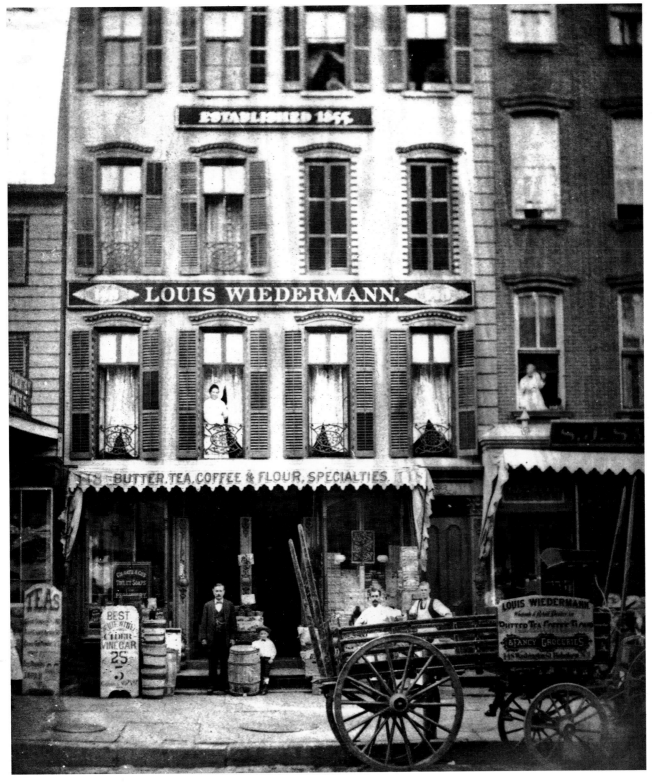

Wiedermann's Groceries at 148 Washington Street did a profitable business in butter, tea, flour, "specialties," and "fancy groceries." In 1885 one might even have them delivered by wagon. Louis Wiedermann was the proprietor for 37 years, and his store was one of the largest in Hudson County. That could be Wiedermann and his son William in front.

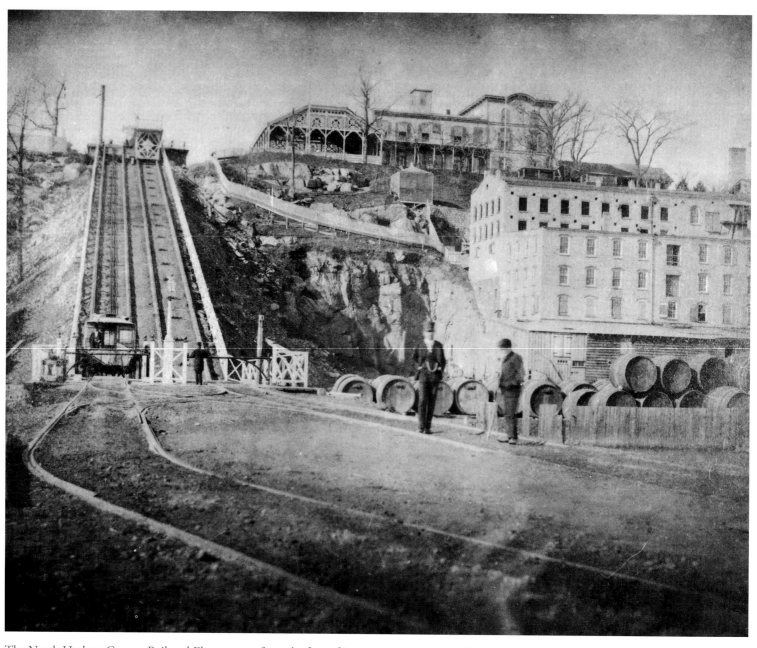

The North Hudson County Railroad Elevator rose from the foot of Ferry Street up to Jersey City Heights. In this view from the 1870s, shortly after the elevator was built, warehouses stand at the top and bottom with goods stacked and waiting for delivery. Note also the horse car and conductor. The elevator was taken apart in 1928.

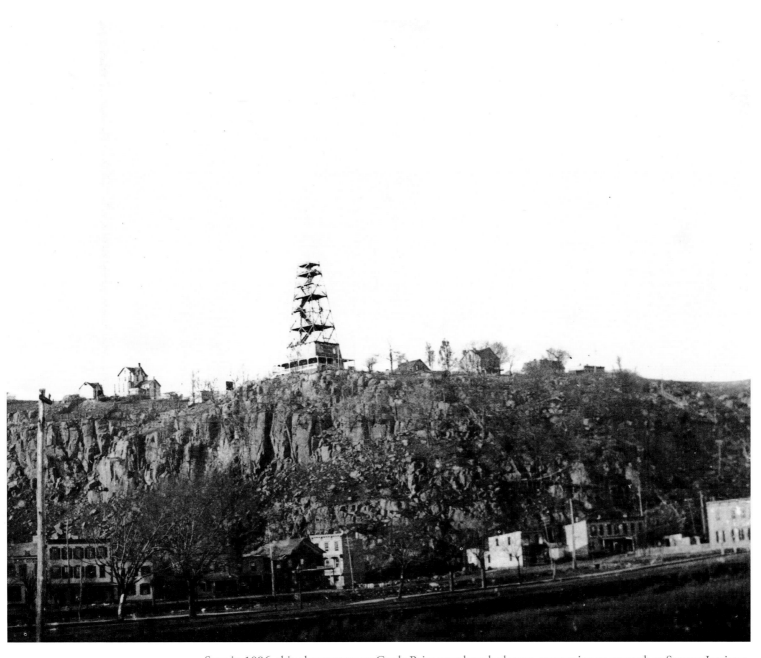

Seen in 1886, this observatory on Castle Point may have had some connection to research at Stevens Institute.

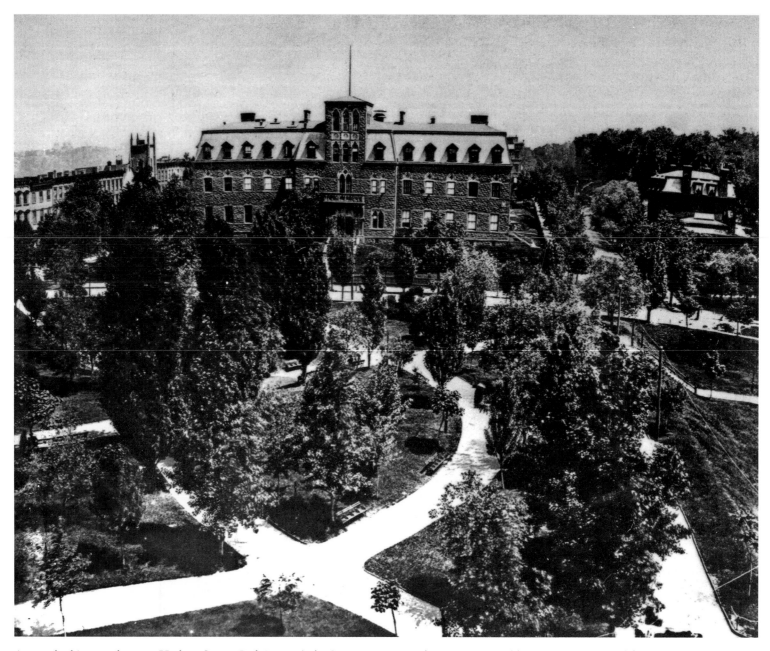

As seen looking north across Hudson Square Park in 1886, the Stevens Institute Administration Building is an imposing edifice, perhaps signifying that education is a solid building block for a student's future.

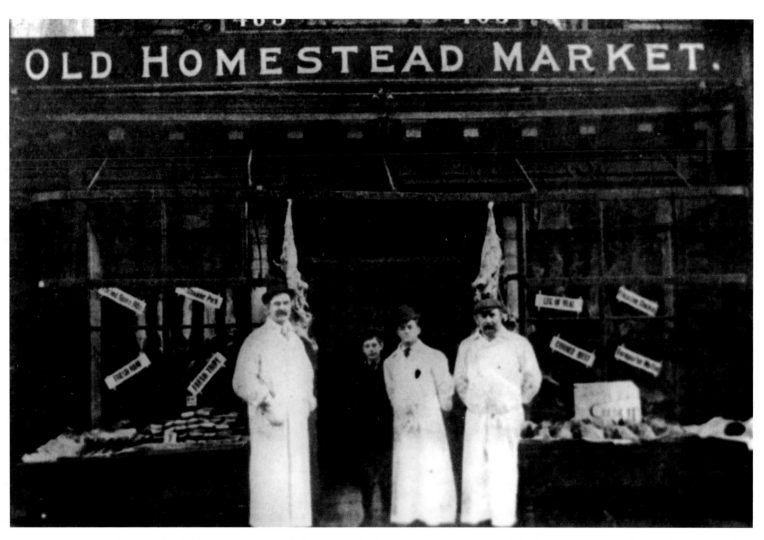

A. E. Strohneir's Old Homestead Market at 463 1st Street was opened in 1888. Wearing butchers' smocks, the three men wait to carve meats for the community and to carve out a living for themselves.

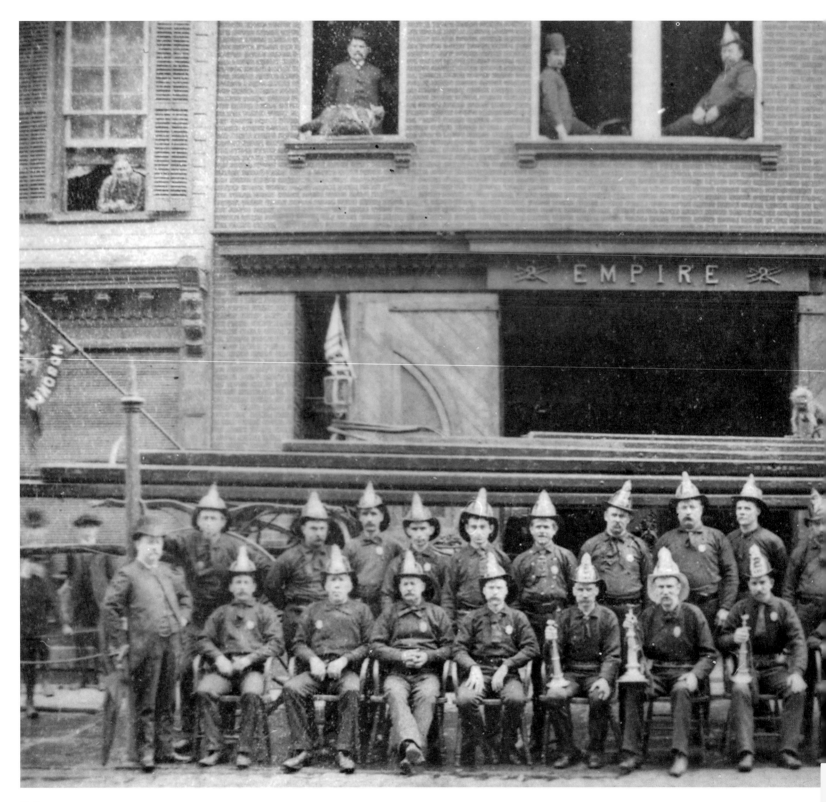

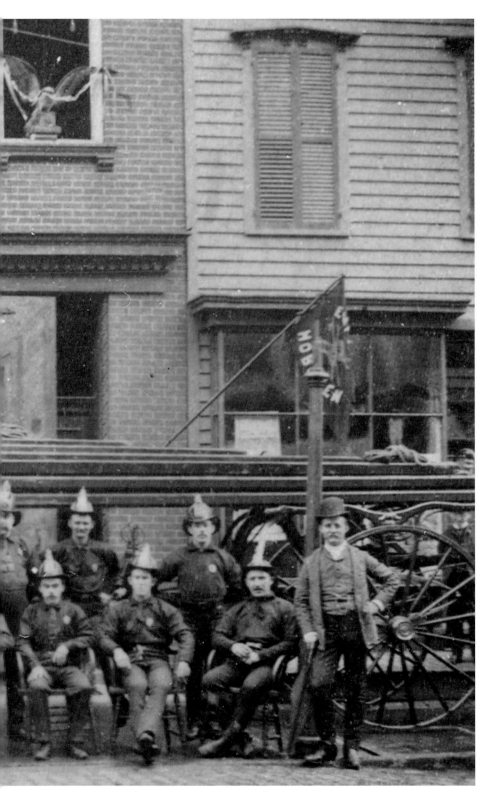

The Empire Hook and Ladder Company No. 2 is out in full regalia and equipment in preparation for the 1888 Decoration Day Parade. The fire house was located on 1st Street near Jefferson Street. Notable are the additional members in the windows and the monkey mascot.

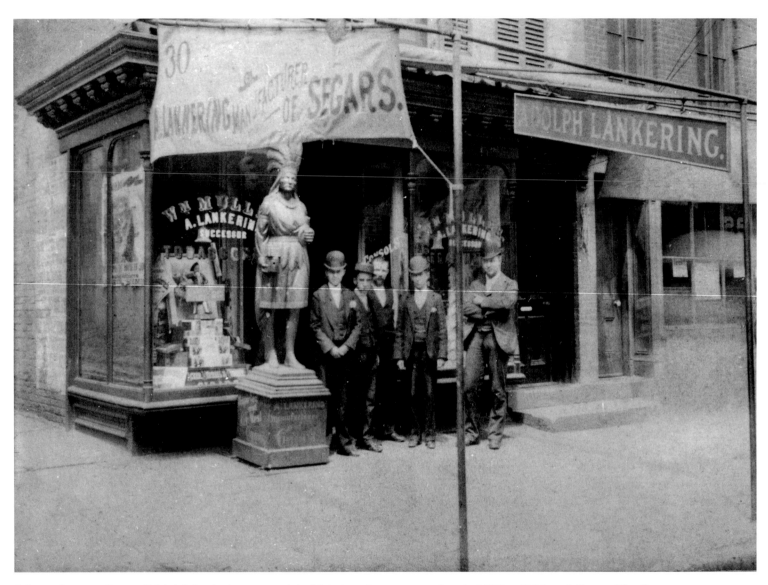

A "manufacturer of segars," Adolph Lankering operated the Hoboken cigar store seen here in 1887 at 30 Newark Street. After first entering the tobacco leaf business in Chicago in 1875, Lankering went east and started a cigar enterprise in Hoboken with his brothers George and Fred. He was elected mayor in 1902, and as a staunch supporter of Governor Woodrow Wilson he was later rewarded with the job of postmaster of Hoboken.

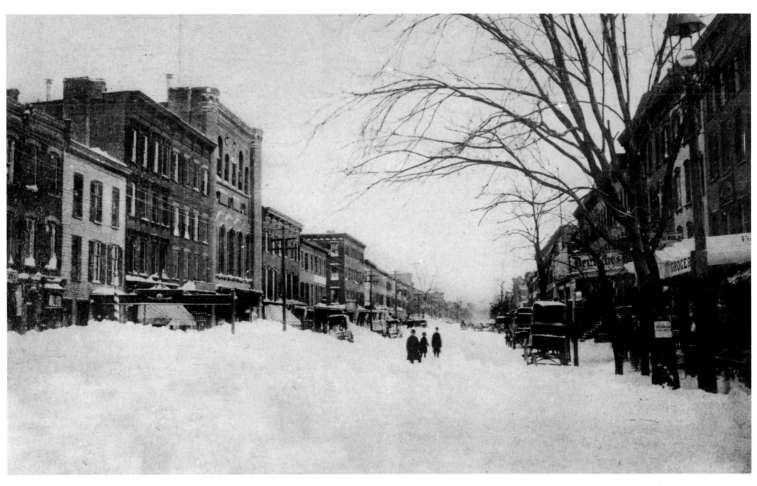

Snowdrifts are piled high on Washington, looking north from 4th Street, after a storm during the winter of 1888.

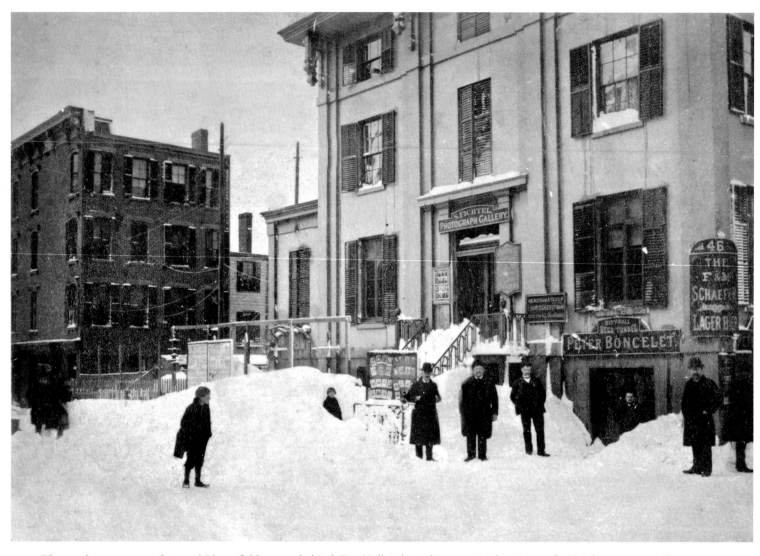

The southwest corner of 1st and Bloomfield streets, behind City Hall, is buried in snow in the winter of 1888, but one can still see a photo gallery and a bar advertising lager beer.

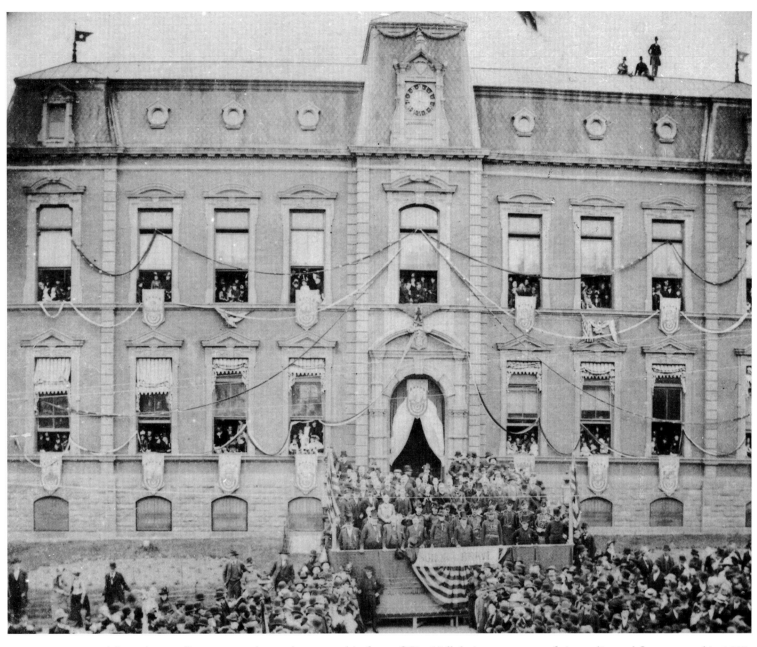

Mayor August Grassman speaks to a large crowd in front of City Hall during a ceremony feting police and fire personnel in 1889. The banner in front has the words "Honor" and "Brave."

Located in Hudson Square Park and seen here about 1889, this monument erected by the people of Hoboken honors the memory of the heroes who didn't return from the Civil War.

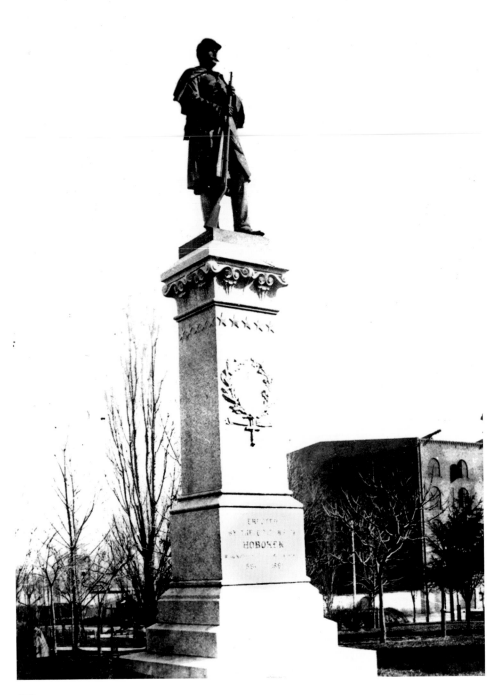

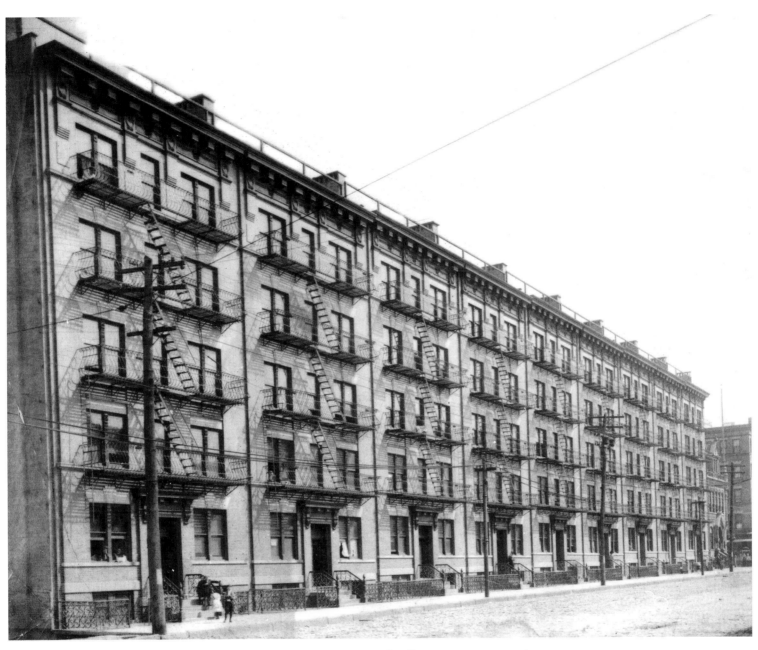

Space was at a premium in 1890s Hoboken, as is illustrated by this photo of Willow Avenue apartment houses.

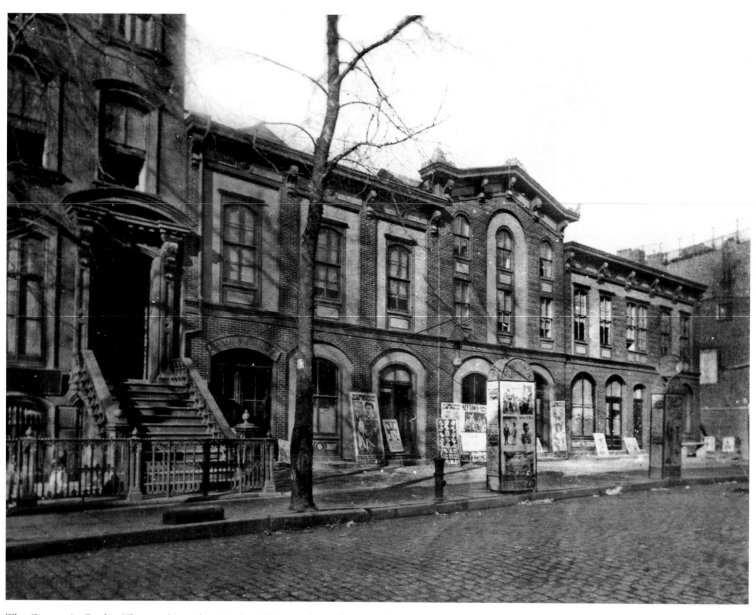

The Germania Garden Theatre shown here in the 1890s was located on Hudson Street between 1st and 2nd streets. It later became the Rialto Theatre. Notice the European-style marquees near the curb.

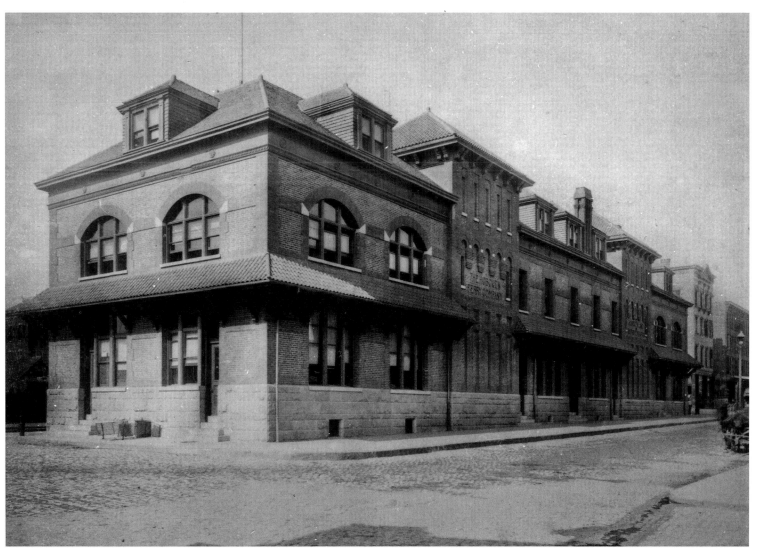

This image is of the rear of the Hoboken Land and Improvement Company in 1890. The company was a private agency in charge of doling out parcels of land in the city for building purposes.

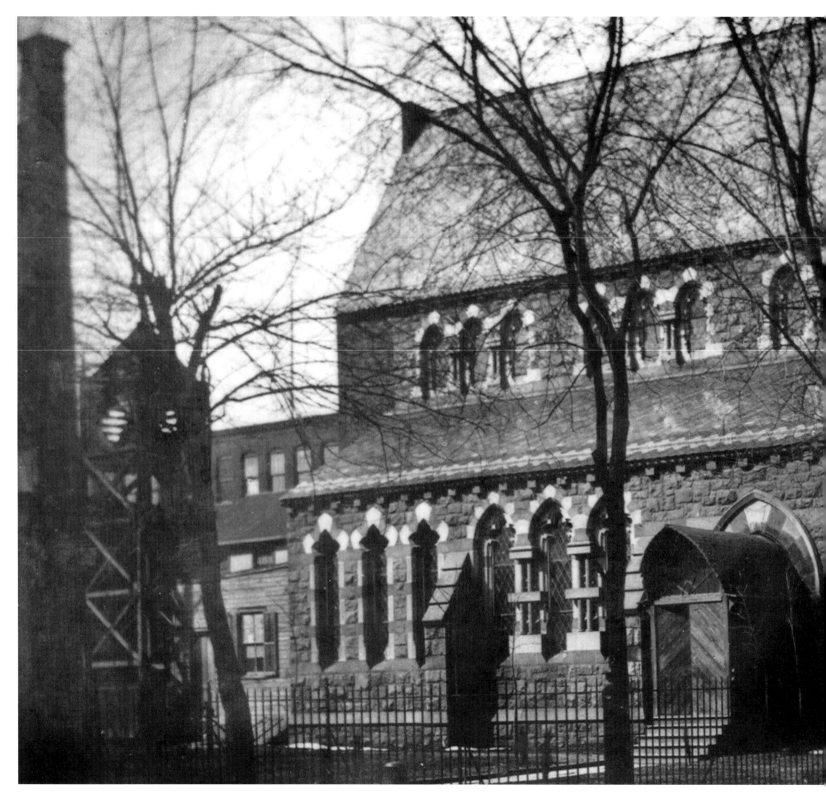

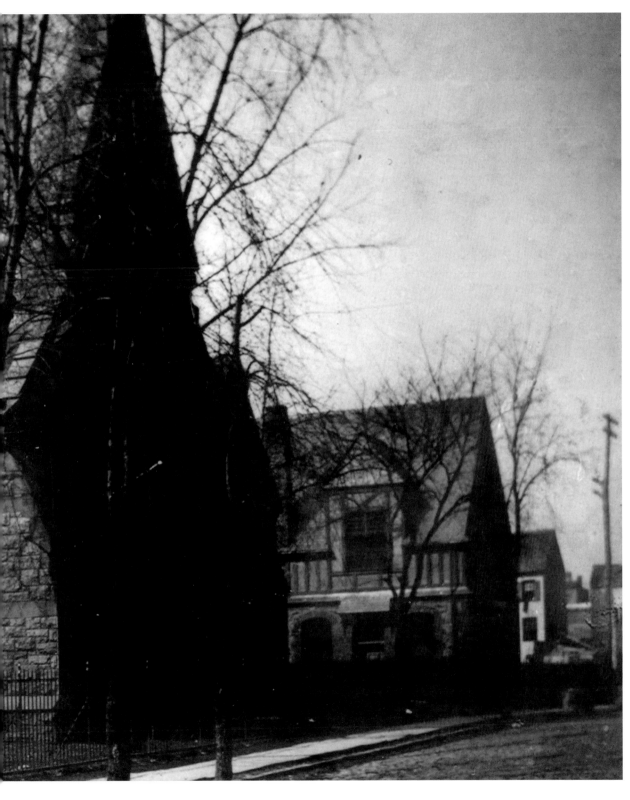

The Church of the Holy Innocents, located on 6th Street between Willow Avenue and Clinton Street, was founded in 1874. Designed by N. V. Halsey Wood, it was endowed by Martha B. Stevens as a memorial to her daughter Julia. The first priest in charge was Reverend Henry F. Hartman; the first rector was C. C. Parsons. The church initially had no pews, just chairs.

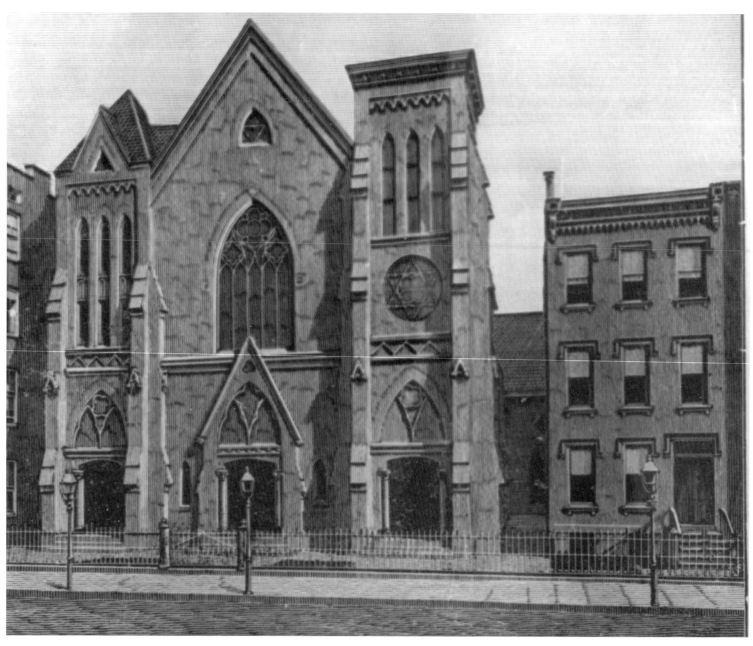

Seen here on Washington Street in 1892, the Methodist Church had relocated from a square at Garden, 4th, 5th, and Willow streets. A structure begun on the square in 1846 collapsed in a storm in 1847. The city claimed the square as public property, and a legal proceeding began which the church lost. A plot on Washington Street was purchased and the church was erected, opening in 1875. The congregation divided into two branches in 1878.

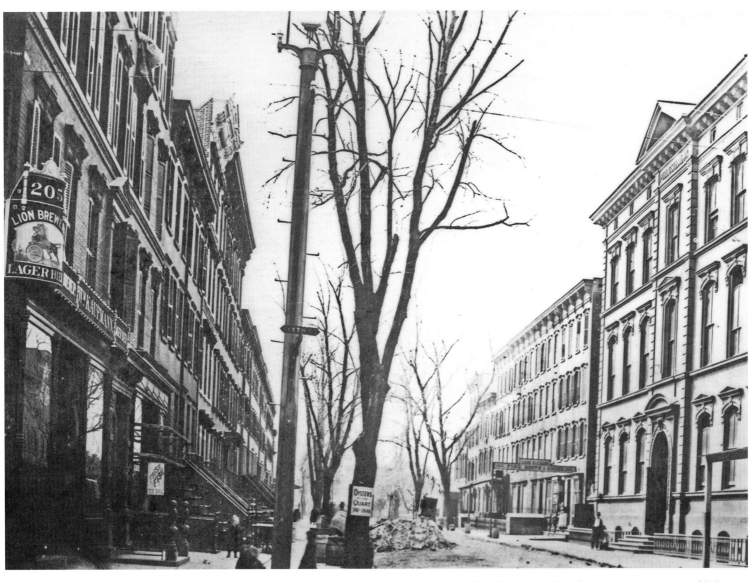

School No. 4 on Park Avenue, at right, is shown here around 1892. The school is within close proximity to an establishment dispensing lager.

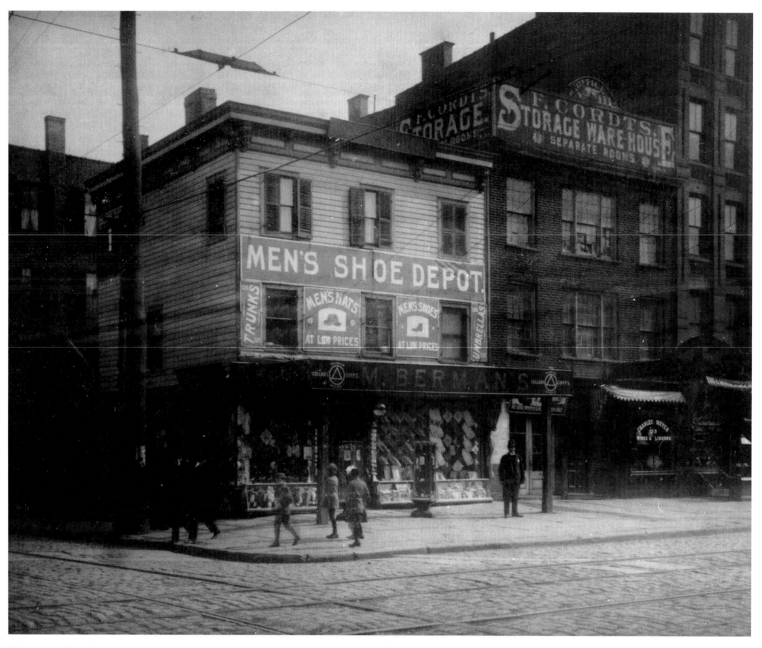

The Men's Shoe Depot, apparently run by M. Berman, was located at 135 Washington Street in 1893. Cordt's Storage Warehouse next door doesn't appear to be much larger than Berman's. The large sidewalk has some foot traffic and is patrolled by the policeman on the beat.

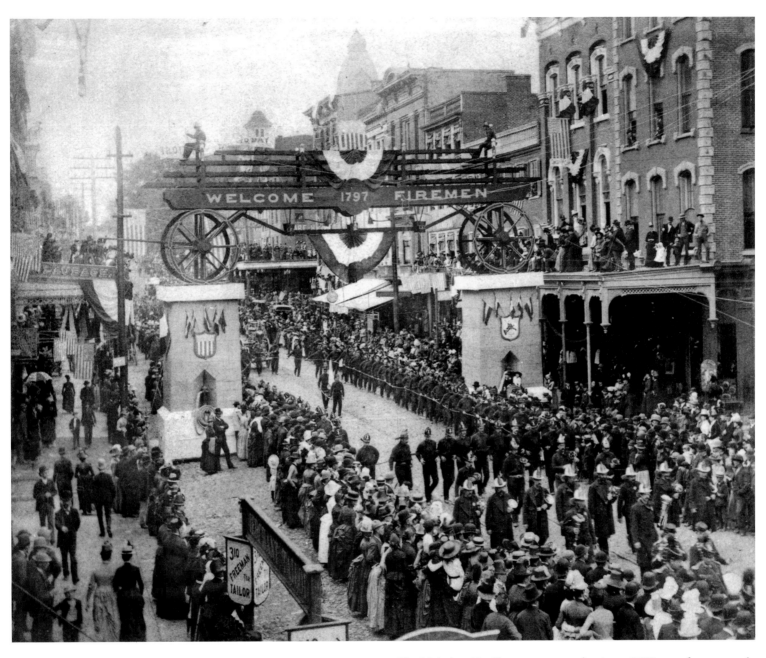

The Hoboken Fire Department marches in an 1897 out-of-town parade.

A group known as L. C. Philibert's Spanish War Veterans indulge and probably swap war stories at a local tavern around 1899. Philibert was a drum major who had his own local drum corps prior to the Spanish-American War.

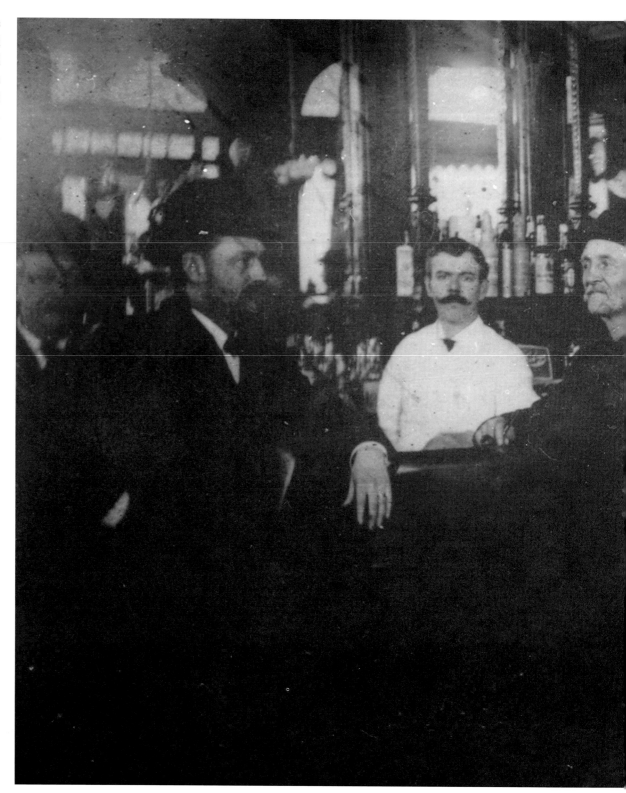

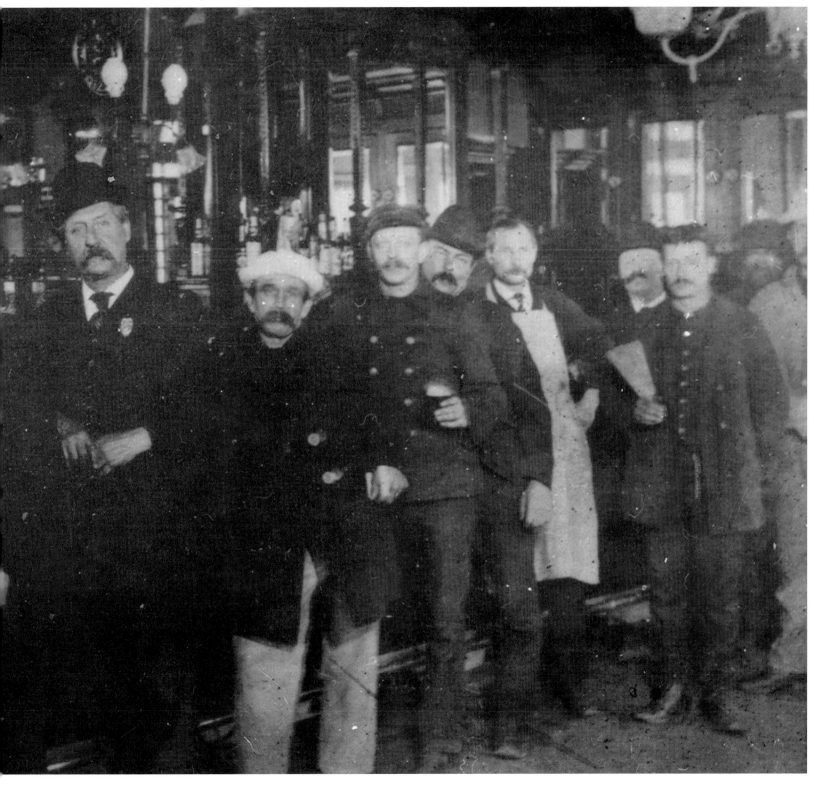

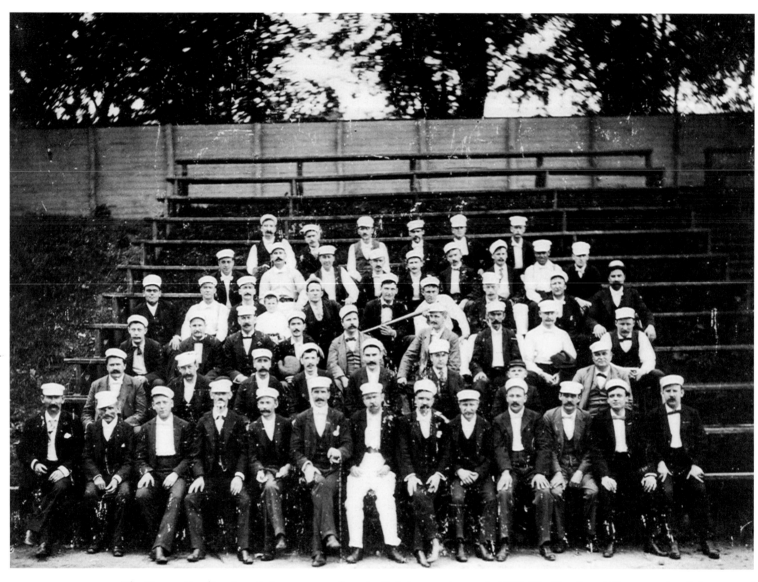

The Pioneer Bowling Association poses outdoors in Hoboken on August 1, 1897. The Dutch and Germans played the game of "ninepins" enthusiastically and brought it with them to the United States.

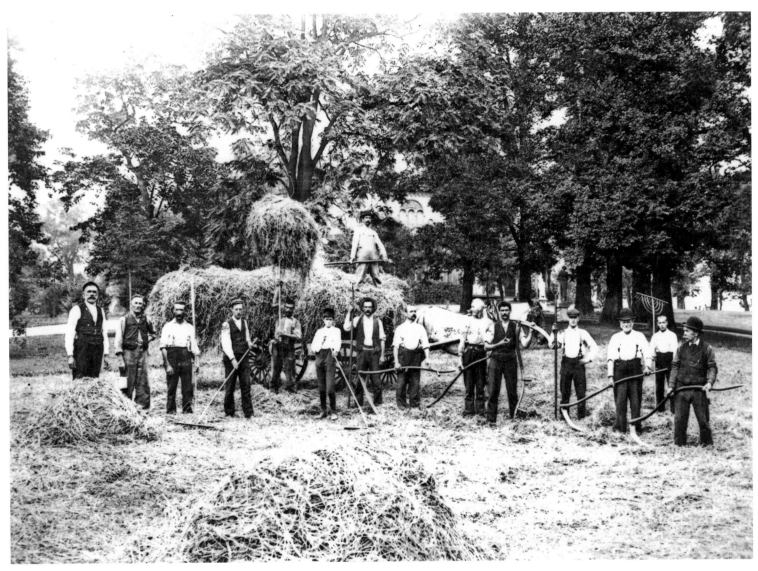

On the Stevens Estate in 1898, workers harvest the hay. The workers would use large scythes and other tools to cut the hay and toss it up onto the horse-drawn wagon.

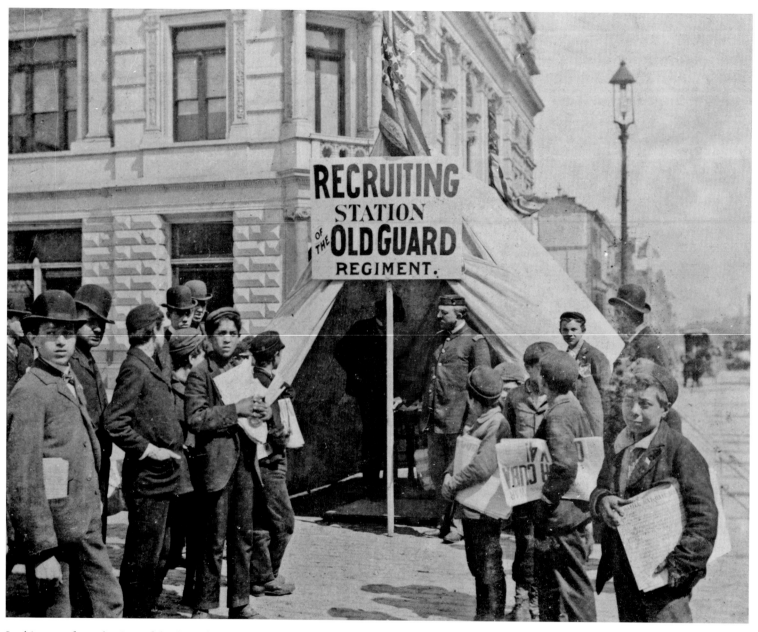

In this scene from the time of the Spanish-American War, newsboys hawk the day's papers in front of a recruiting tent set up for enlisting Hoboken men into the Old Guard Regiment. An officer is out front to welcome volunteers.

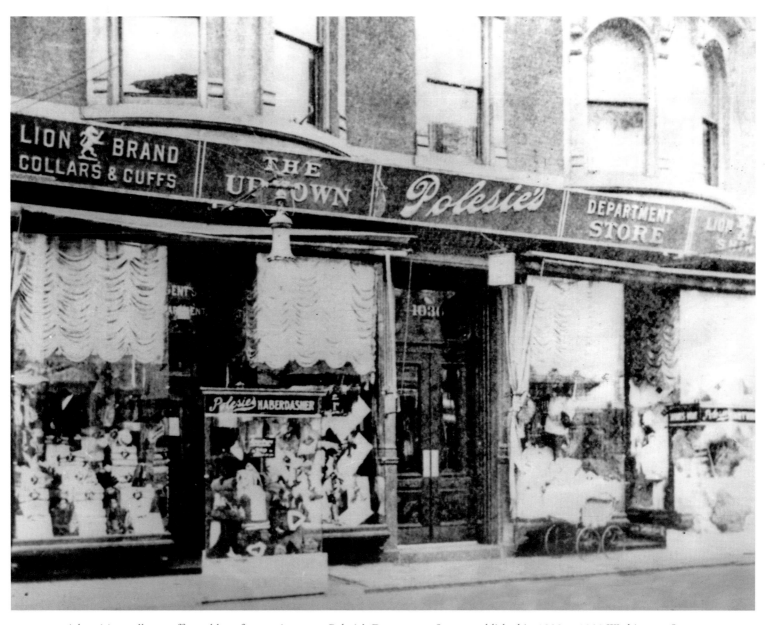

Advertising collars, cuffs, and hats for evening wear, Polesie's Department Store, established in 1898 at 1030 Washington Street, appears to have been an "uptown" store. Polesie is a large marshy area in Poland, indicating the store may have been operated by a Pole or Slavic owner.

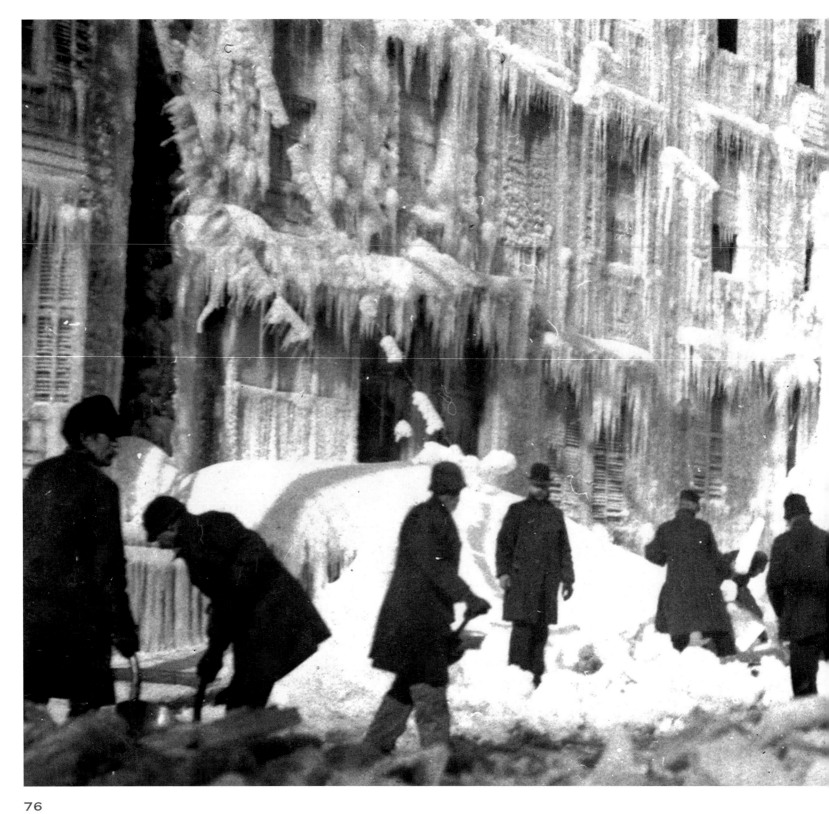

76

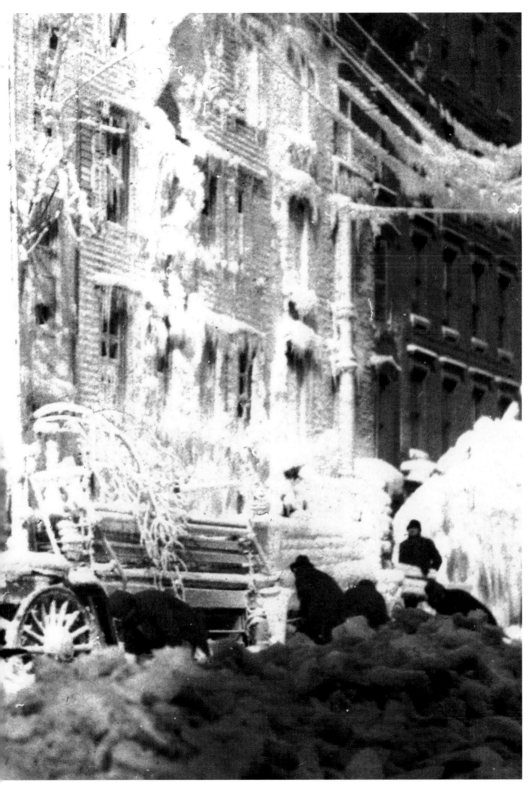

Fire fighters struggled in the freezing cold to battle a blaze at 308-312 Clinton Street on February 8, 1899. Here men are clearing away ice the next day. One fire wagon is shown, as well as what appears to be a wagon completely covered in ice at right.

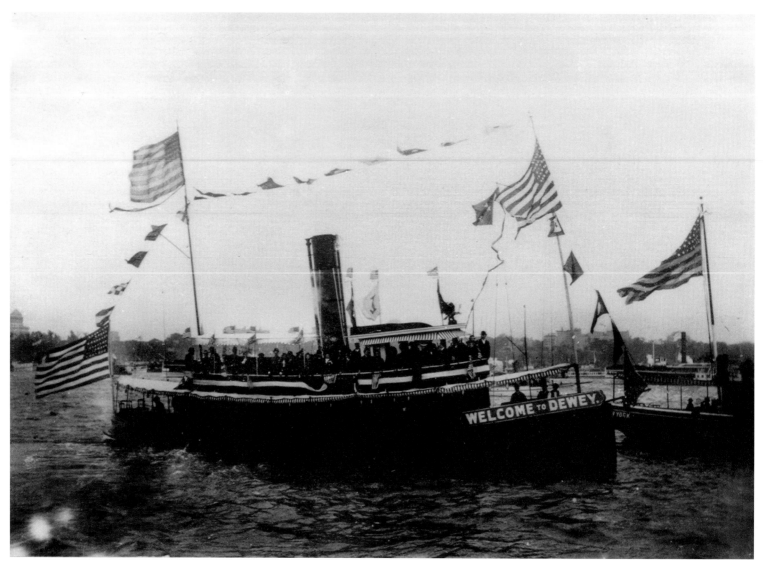

On September 30, 1899, a contingent from Hoboken boarded craft to welcome home Admiral George Dewey from his Manila campaign during the Spanish-American War. Flags flap wildly in the breeze. This was also the occasion of the first Marconi wireless broadcast for commercial purposes in America, reaching from out at sea to Sandy Hook, New Jersey, and on to the New York City papers.

PORT CITY IN A NEW CENTURY

(1900–1929)

The population of Hoboken grew from 9,000 in 1860 to nearly 60,000 in 1900. Most were immigrants working hard for someone else or taking chances on themselves in their own businesses. Hotels, saloons, dealers in building and shipping supplies, and public services all needed men and women.

Transportation was vital. Numerous ferries were established. The Hoboken Terminal, built in 1907 by Kenneth M. Murchison and featuring a beaux-arts design that included Tiffany stained glass, became a major rail hub and ferry terminal; the main destination was New York City. Rail lines into Hoboken increased as more shipping and manufacturing facilities were built. The Keuffel & Esser Manufacturing Company built an enormous facility in 1906, and this was typical. Operations like these meant more jobs for more people, and Hoboken continued growing.

Joy rarely comes without heartache, however. In a small city like Hoboken, with crowded tenements, overflowing warehouses, and larger and larger ships arriving, the threat of fire was constant. In 1900, the North German Lloyd pier caught fire and the flames quickly spread to other ships and warehouses. The fire burned for three days at a cost of more than 300 lives and $5 million in damages. The entire city went into mourning, but the resilient people worked on. This resiliency was born of foreigners wanting to become Americans—imagine the feelings of those entering the harbor when they flocked to the side of a ship where they could glimpse the Statue of Liberty through a morning mist.

War clouds covered Europe by 1914. The start of World War I threatened our peace and made the German population of Hoboken uneasy. The United States' entry in 1917 made the city an integral part of the war effort. The American Expeditionary Force led by General John J. "Black Jack" Pershing used Hoboken piers as its main embarkation point. Sadly, it was also the final destination for brave soldiers who lost their lives "over there." The city was immortalized with the famous slogan "Heaven, Hell, or Hoboken," spoken by the doughboys as they sailed. Meanwhile, the German piers were confiscated, parts of the city were placed under martial law, and Germans were forcibly removed to Ellis Island.

After the war, Hoboken remained a vital port city, even through the Great Depression, partly due to the strength of the shipbuilding industry. It would remain so while war clouds once again darkened Europe.

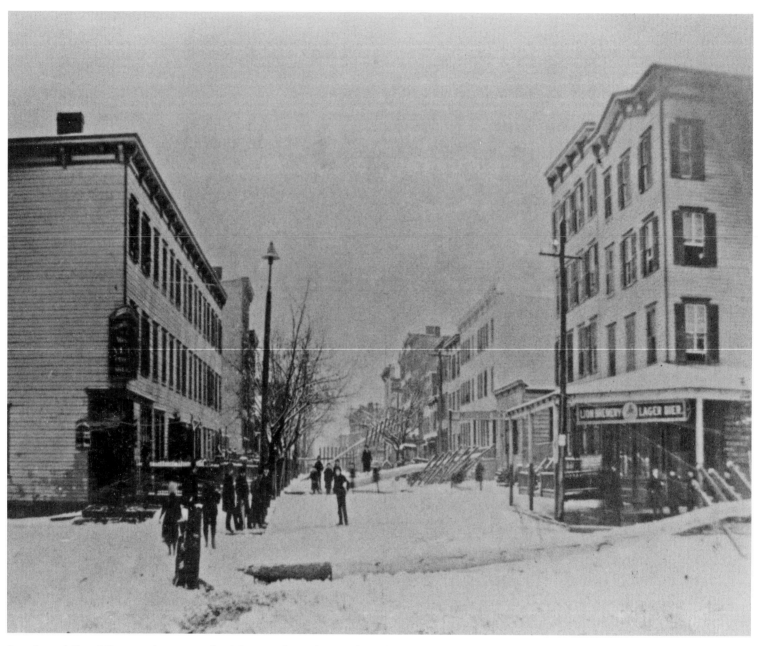

Snowbound Grand Street at the corner of 3rd Street is shown here in the early 1900s. Children playing and people out walking are enjoying the snow day. The closeness of the mostly wood structures seen here made for good friends but dangerous quarters.

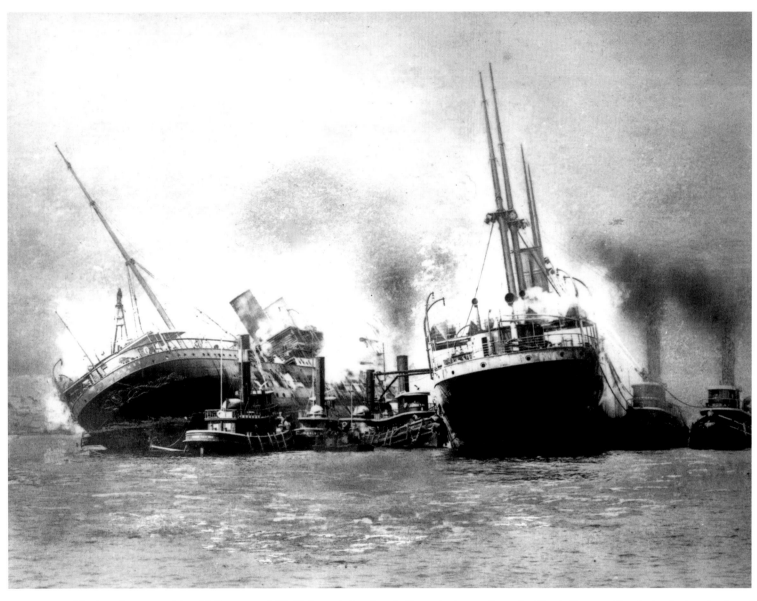

The burning steamships SS *Bremen* and SS *Main* are being frantically pushed away from the North German Lloyd pier during the fire of June 30, 1900. The cause of the fire is still unknown. Also damaged were the *Kaiser Wilhelm der Grosse* and the *Saale*. The scene was chaotic, with wind-driven flames burning ropes and setting the ships adrift, and tugboats scrambling to stop them for fear of the fire spreading beyond the adjacent piers.

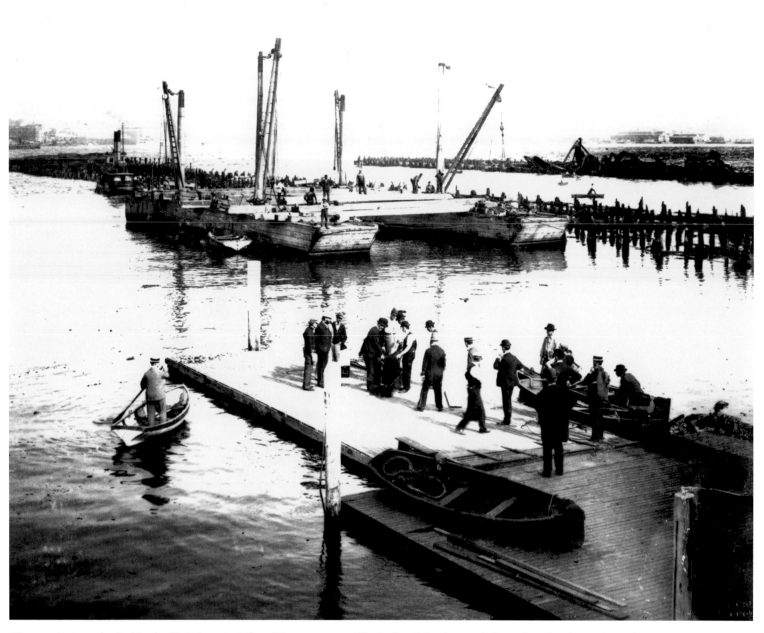

Close to 400 people died in the Hoboken dock fire of June 30, 1900. The hulks of the damaged ships glowed red into the night after the fire was out. Here men search for bodies of those who perished. The excavation of the ships, as part of the search, became the mission of many volunteers. Amazingly, some survivors were found and pulled out alive, having been trapped in safe pockets shielded from the flames.

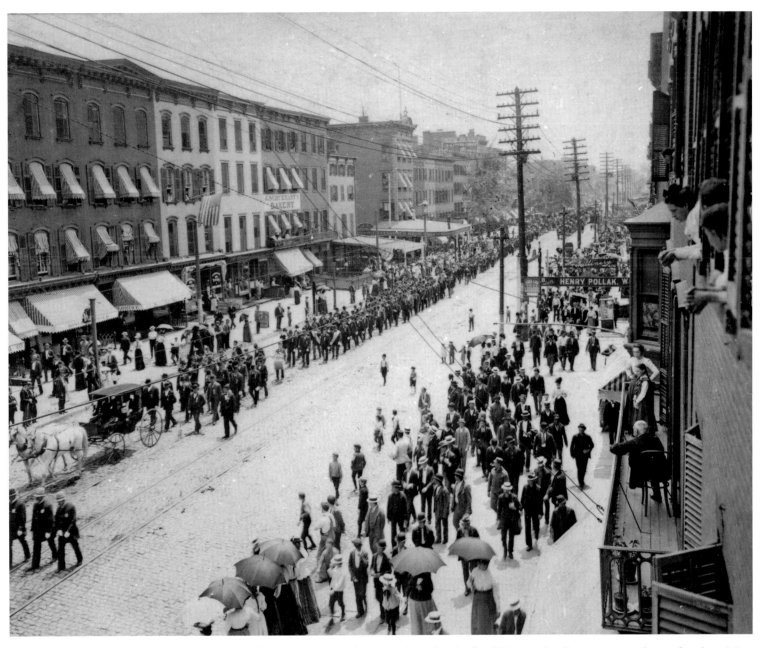

Onlookers on Washington Street watch a funeral procession that took place after the fire. This was the climax to a tumultuous few days. More than one million people in the surrounding area witnessed the fire, which was documented by photographers and journalists alike. The North German Lloyd line was not just an employer in Hoboken; its sailors and workmen availed themselves of the local German population and endeared themselves to the community. It was a tragic loss. The line, still operating, is called the Hapag/Lloyd Line.

This is an early 1900s photo of the First Dutch Reformed Church on Bloomfield Street.

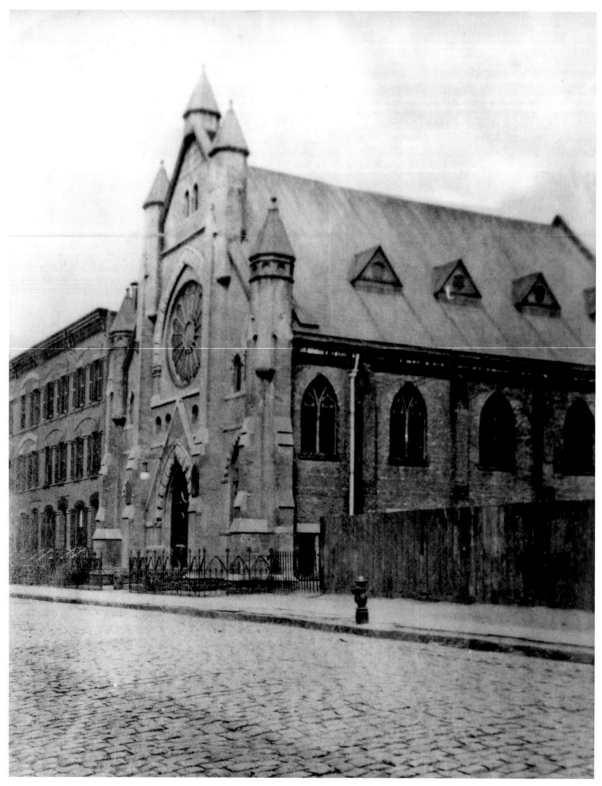

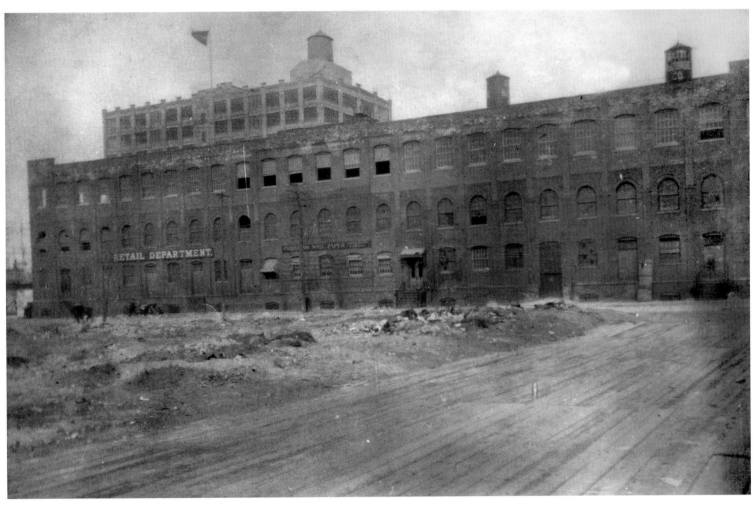

The Gatti-McQuade Company manufactured thread from linen. This building seen in 1909 was on Madison Street. The company experienced its share of controversy, first becoming embroiled in a customs fight over tax paid on linen, then in a third-party labor and manufacturing suit with the Eagle Paper Box Company that is still cited in case law today. The company went bankrupt in the early 1920s.

This grand structure housed Hoboken Engine Company No. 2 at 1313 Washington Street. The building still stands and is still home to an active engine company. Ladder Company No. 1 has been added.

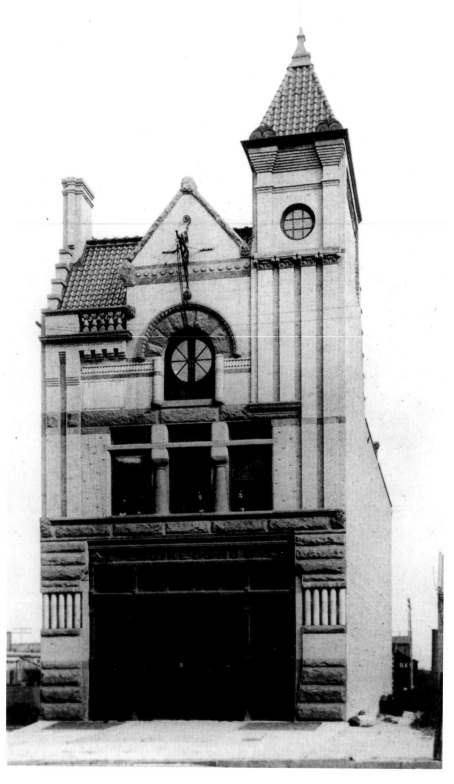

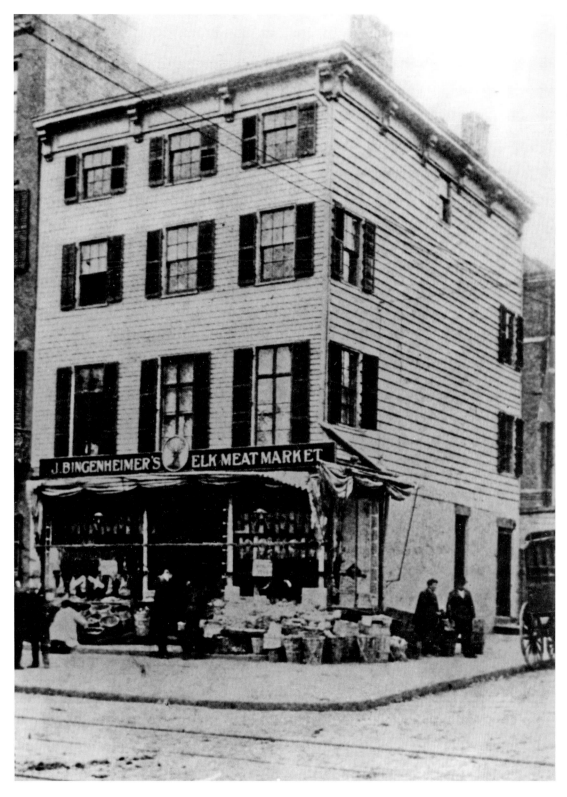

J. Bingenheimer's Elk Meat Market was started in 1900 at 401 Washington Street. A typical turn-of-the-century store with wares sold inside and out, the market and others of its ilk were precursors to the farmer's markets of today.

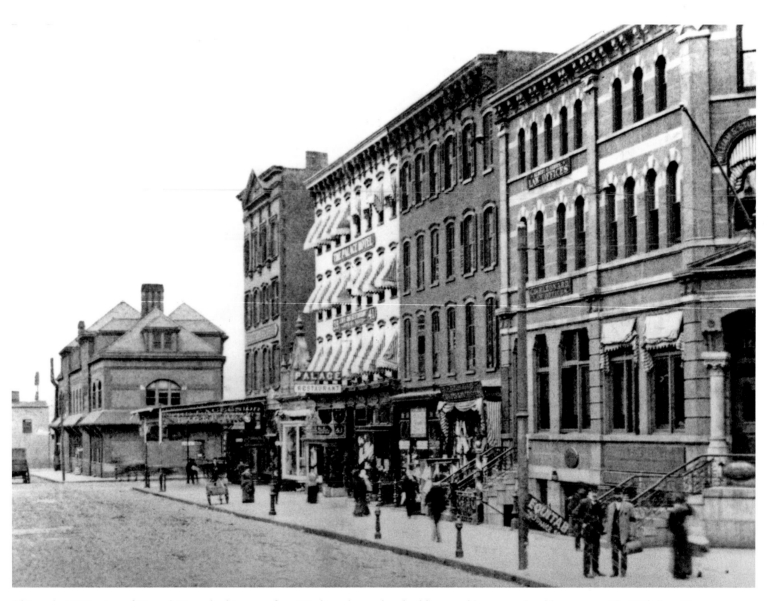

This early 1900s view of Newark Street looking east from Hudson shows close buildings and basement-level businesses. The Hoboken First Bank on the corner was torn down in 1912 to be replaced by another bank.

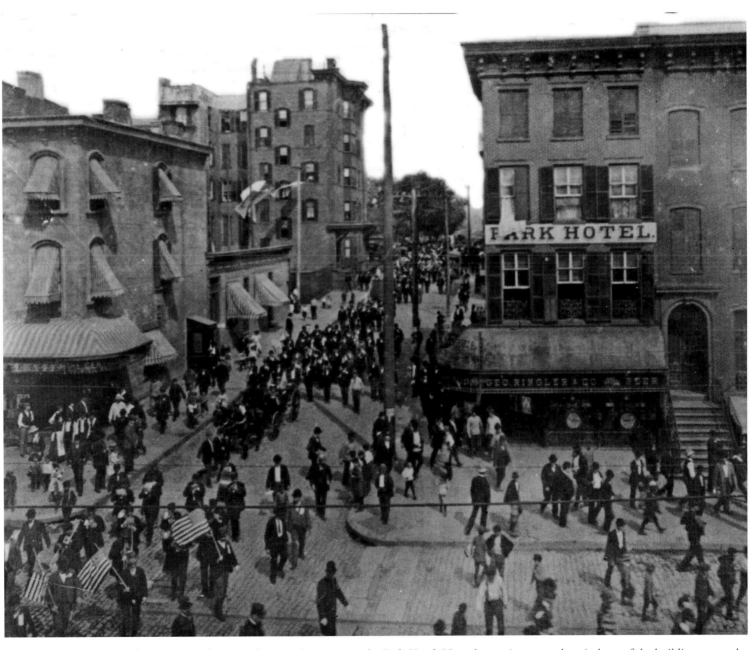

An early 1900s parade on Washington Street passes the Park Hotel. Note the awnings over the windows of the building across the street, placed to keep the hot sun out since air-conditioning was not yet available.

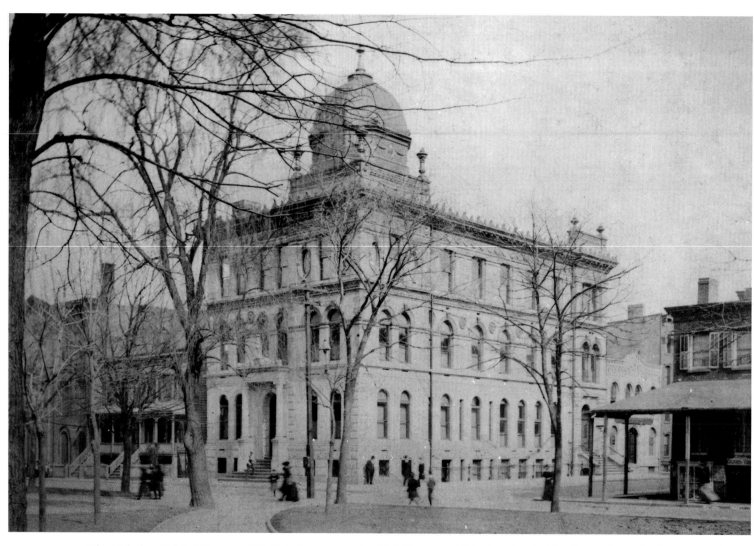

The Hoboken Public Library at 500 Park Avenue was the third library established under the New Jersey General Library Act of 1894, following those of Paterson and Newark. The cornerstone was laid April 14, 1896, and the library opened its doors on April 5, 1897. Seen here a few years after opening, it is still in operation at the same location.

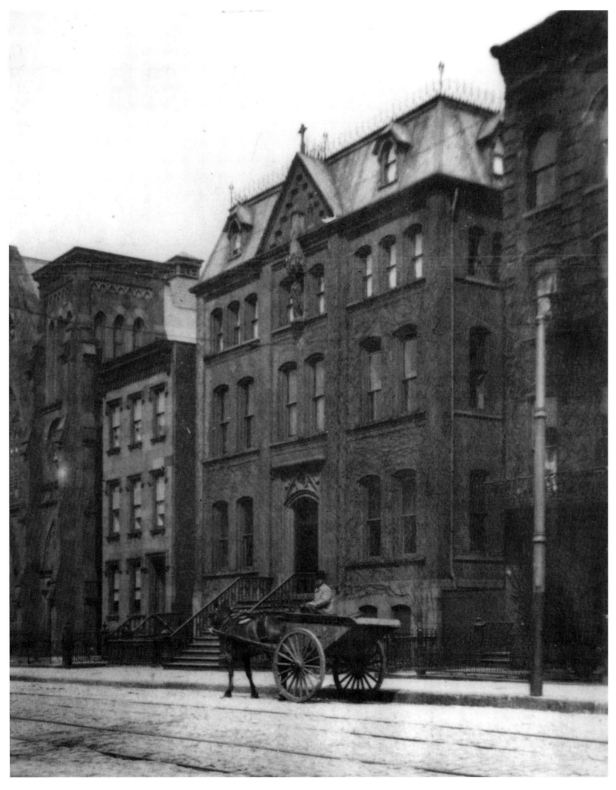

Sacred Heart Academy, located at 713 Washington Street, is a Catholic school for young women administered by the Sisters of Charity of St. Elizabeth. Seen here around 1900, it opened in 1868 and is still in operation.

This early 1900s photo shows the Gayety Theatre on upper Washington Street. Adjacent to the theatre in the frame building was the Quartet Club, whose membership included nearly every prominent member of the German-American community in Hudson County.

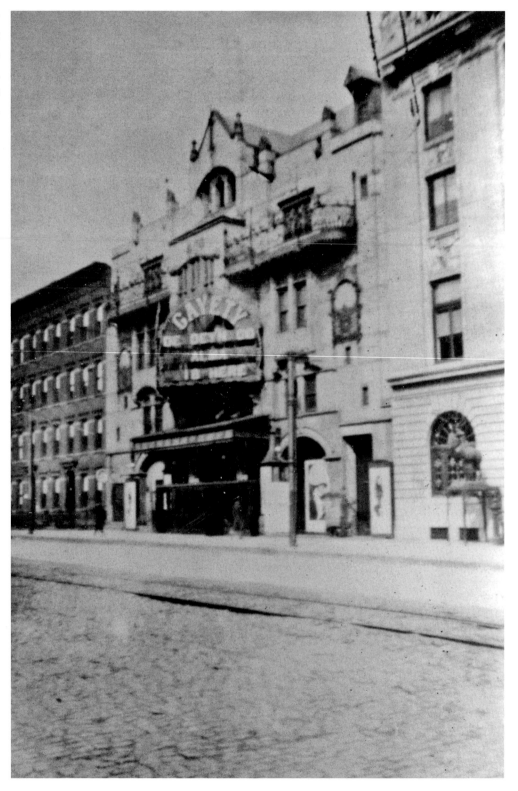

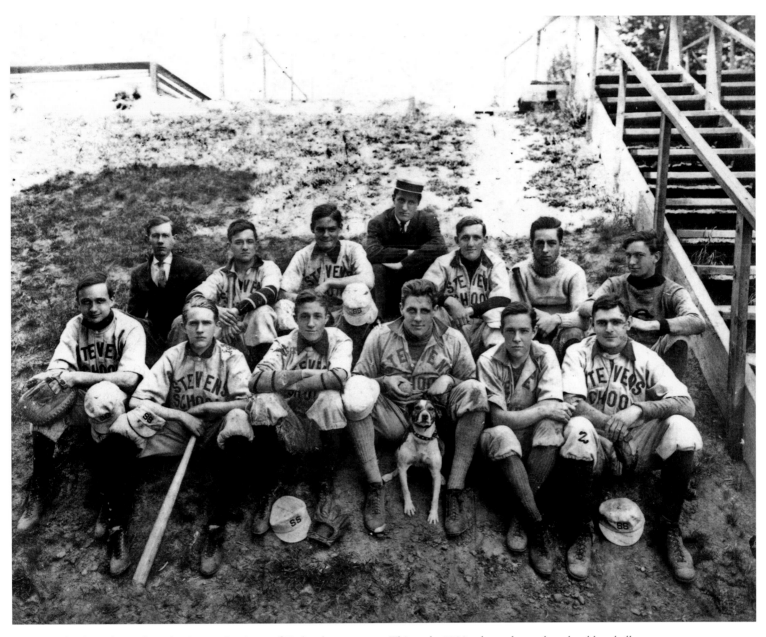

Stevens School was located on the Stevens Institute of Technology campus. This early 1900s photo shows the school baseball team, including its canine mascot, near the Castle Point steps.

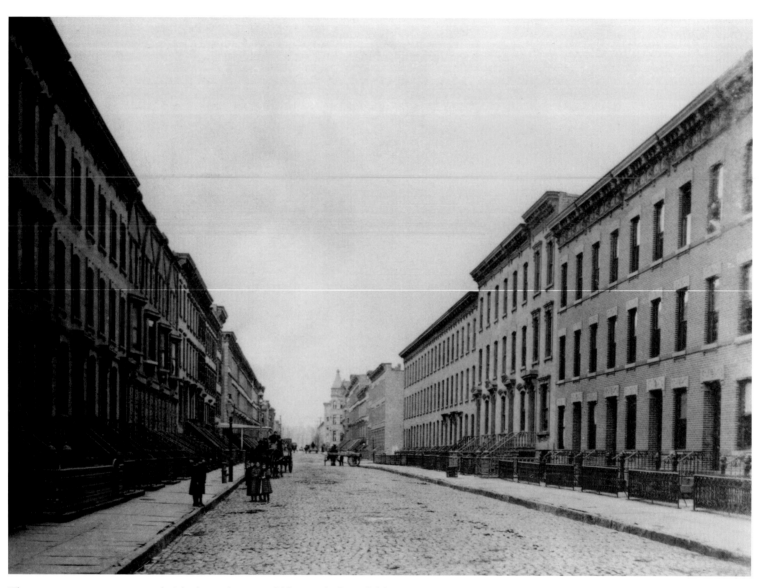

Three-story tenements are sandwiched together on cobblestoned Bloomfield Street between 9th and 10th in this early 1900s view.

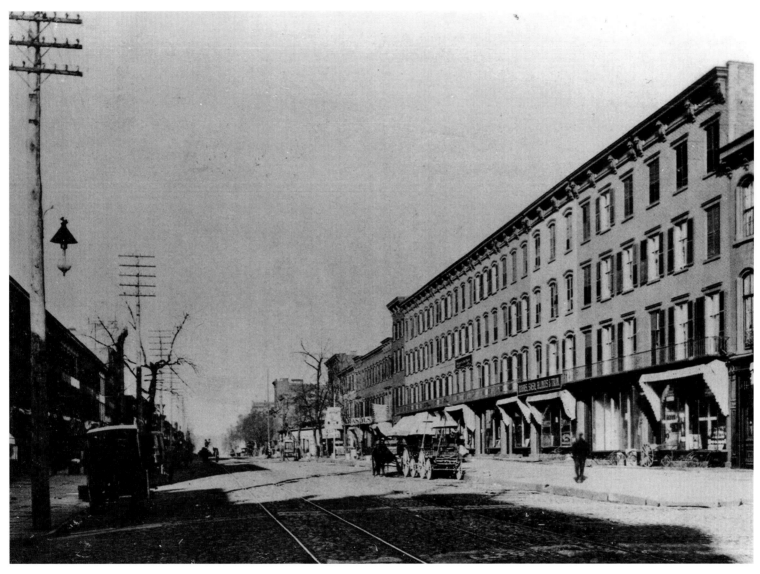

Storefronts, apartments, and horse-drawn carts line sunny Washington Street in the early 1900s. Note the trolley tracks and telephone poles signifying a modernizing city.

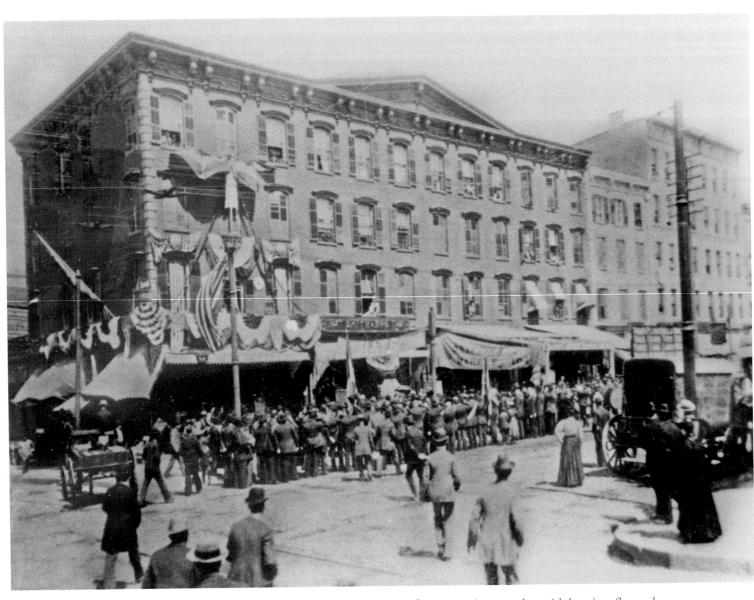

The Beekman Store's grand opening at 1st and Washington streets in 1901 was a festive occasion complete with bunting, flags, a large crowd, and a bow on the building.

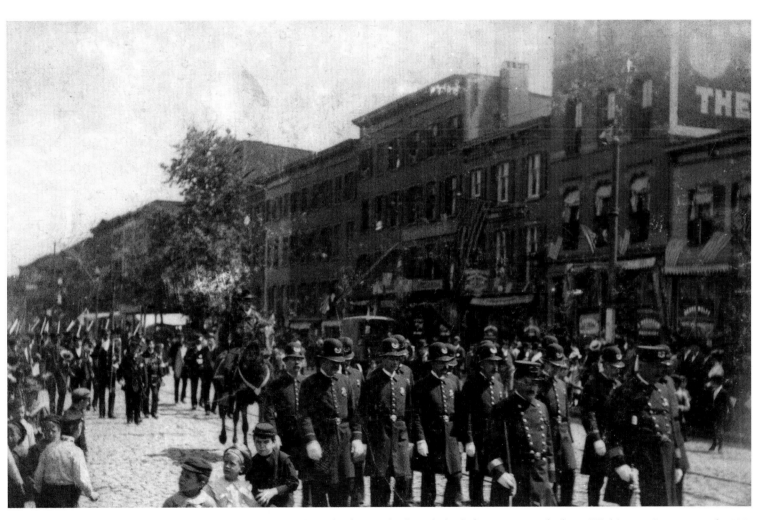

Police Chief Hayes leads Hoboken's finest in a parade down Washington Street around 1902.

The Castle, sometimes called Castle Stevens, was the residence of Edwin A. Stevens, founder and benefactor of Stevens Institute of Technology. Purchased by Colonel John Stevens and rebuilt in 1854, the house was turned over to the Stevens Institute on May 27, 1911. A year later it became a 45-room dormitory and meeting place for students. The building was demolished in 1959.

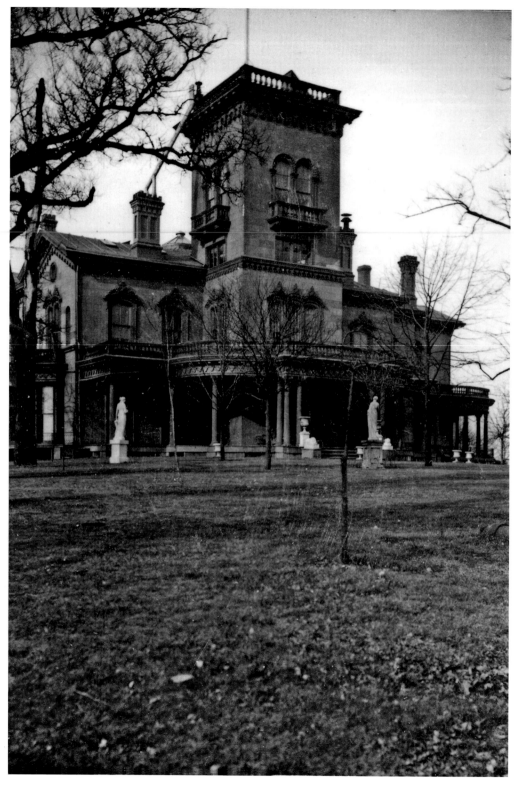

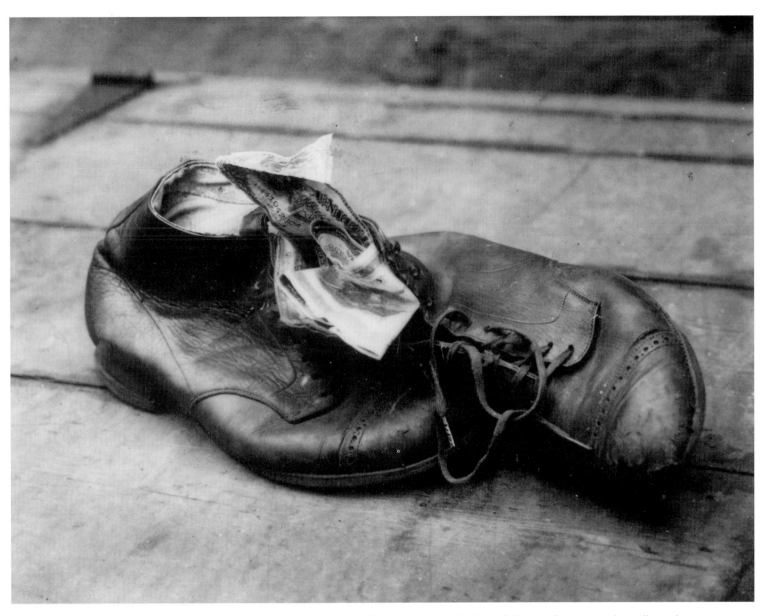

On January 30, 1905, fire broke out in a third-floor linen room of the Colonial Hotel at 59 Newark Street. Flames spread rapidly, and 12 people were killed. A man named Walters who had hidden money in his shoe was able to recover it at the police station with his $450 still intact.

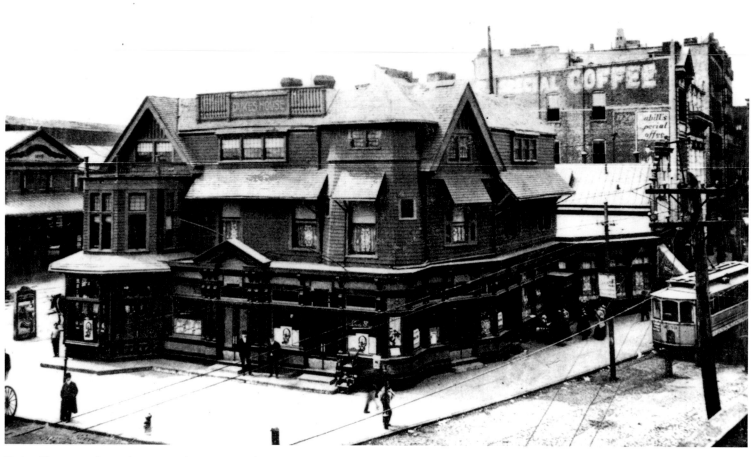

Dukes House was located on Newark Street near the Hoboken Ferry. Owned by businessman Henry Ranken, it was a noted tavern that drew clientele from boxer John L. Sullivan to millionaire William K. Vanderbilt. The tavern burned in an August 7, 1905, fire that started on the piers of the Delaware, Lackawanna, and Western Railroad a few blocks away. Four ferries were consumed in the flames that spread to shacks, warehouses, and eventually Dukes.

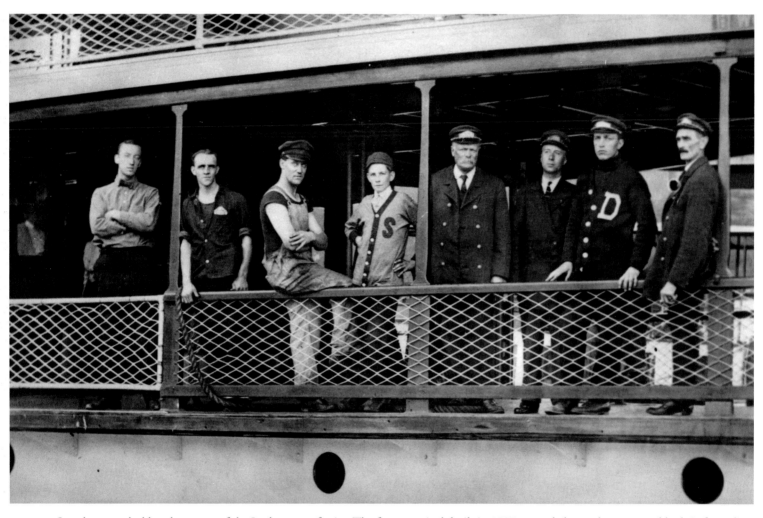

Seen here are deckhands on one of the Lackawanna ferries. The ferry terminal, built in 1907, extended over the water and had six ferry slips, and tracks for up to 14 trains. With business possibilities abounding after the turn of the century, the need for more ferries to New York was realized.

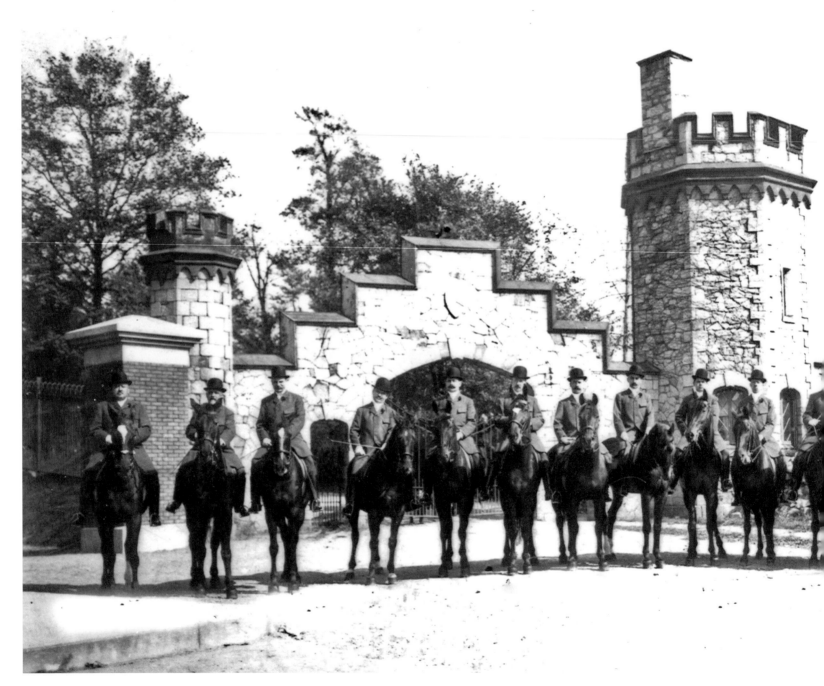

102

Fresh air and exercise were the order of the day for these members of the Hoboken Riding Club, seen in front of the Stevens Castle gate in 1904. Riding was popular in the heights above the Hudson River. The Hexamer Riding Club and the German Riding Club were two more clubs in the area. They frequently joined New York clubs for trips to the Adirondacks.

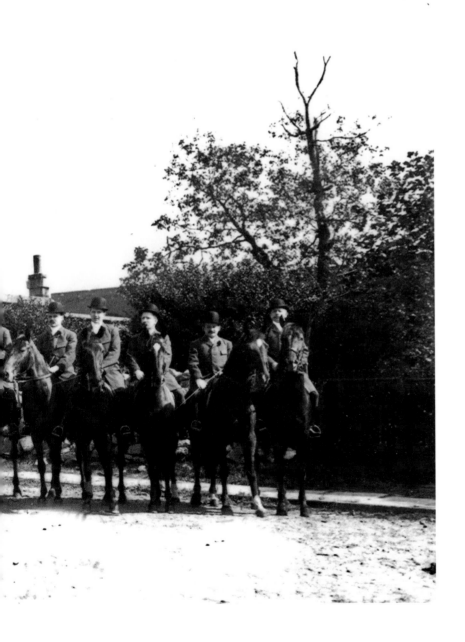

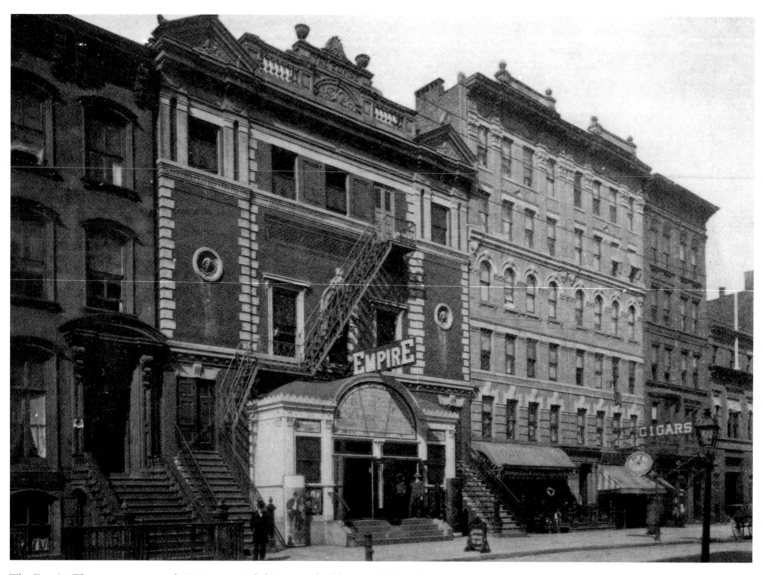

The Empire Theatre, seen around 1905, occupied this ornate building on Hudson Street.

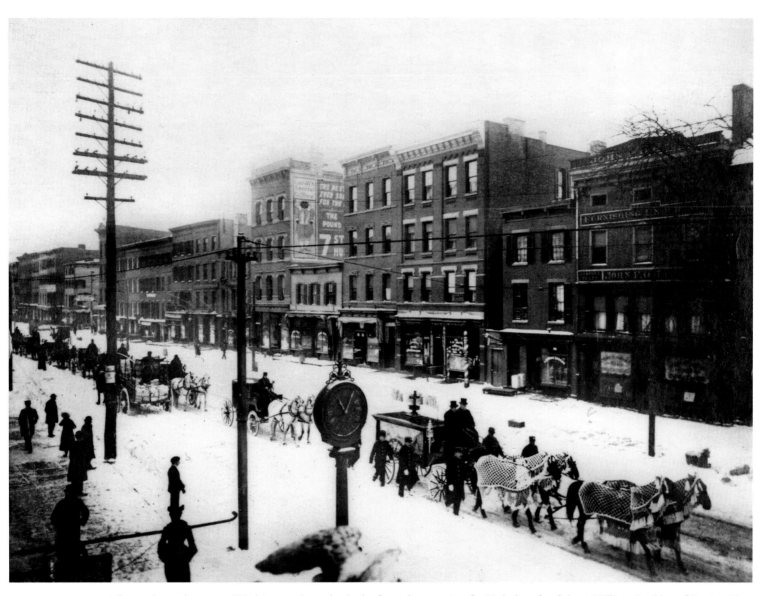

A horse-drawn hearse on Washington Street leads the funeral procession for Hoboken fire fighter William Buckley of Engine Five. Buckley perished in a blaze at the Elysian Supply Company Factory on January 2, 1905.

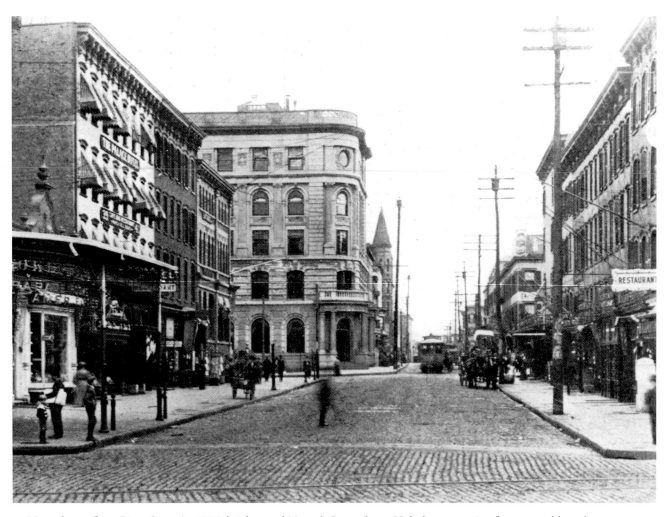

Viewed west from River Street in 1905, brick-paved Newark Street shows Hoboken as a mix of many worlds and many scenes, a turn-of-the-century mini-metropolis.

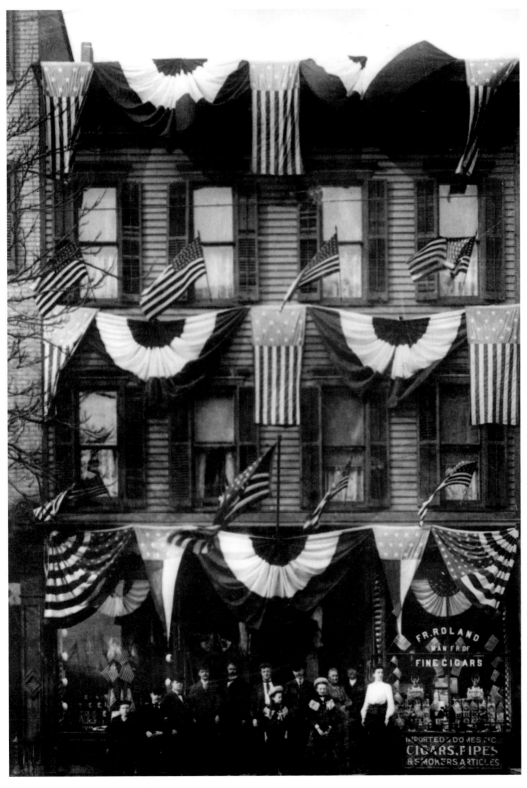

Located on 1st Street, the Roland cigar store is outfitted for a March 28, 1905, celebration of the 50th anniversary of Hoboken's incorporation.

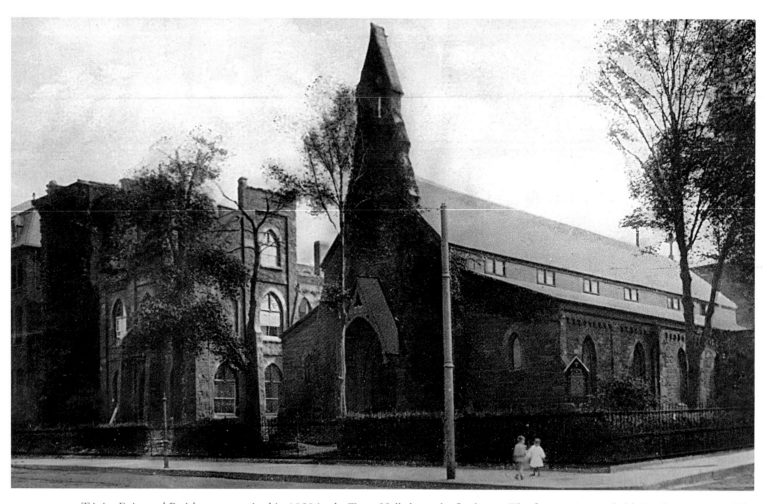

Trinity Episcopal Parish was organized in 1853 in the Town Hall above the fire house. The first service was held October 18, 1853. The current church, located at 7th and Washington streets and seen here in 1905, was finished in 1856. Reverend N. W. Camp was the first rector.

The increasing bustle of twentieth-century Hoboken can be sensed in this 1905 street scene on Washington near 3rd.

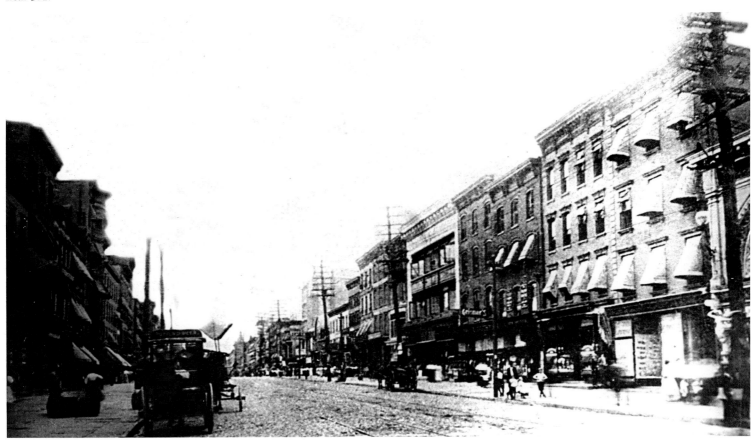

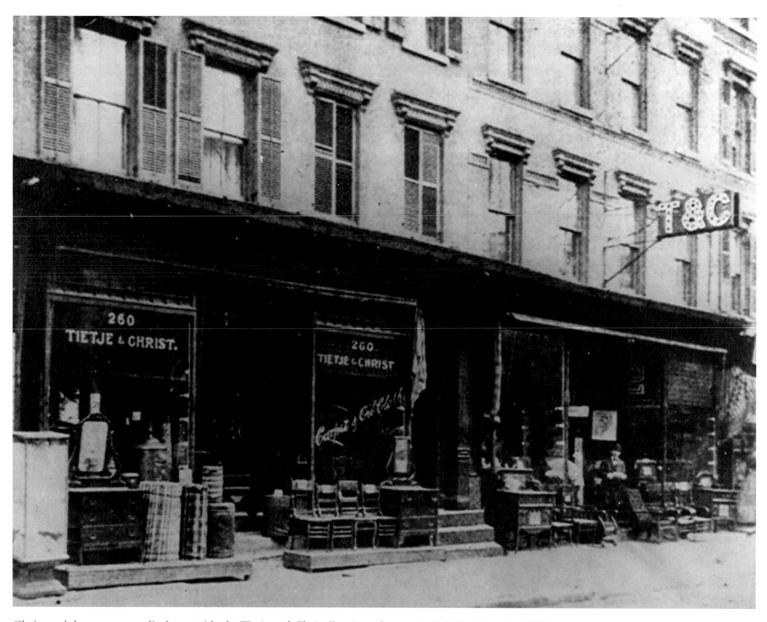

Chairs and dressers are on display outside the Tietje and Christ Furniture Store at 258-60 1st Street in 1906.

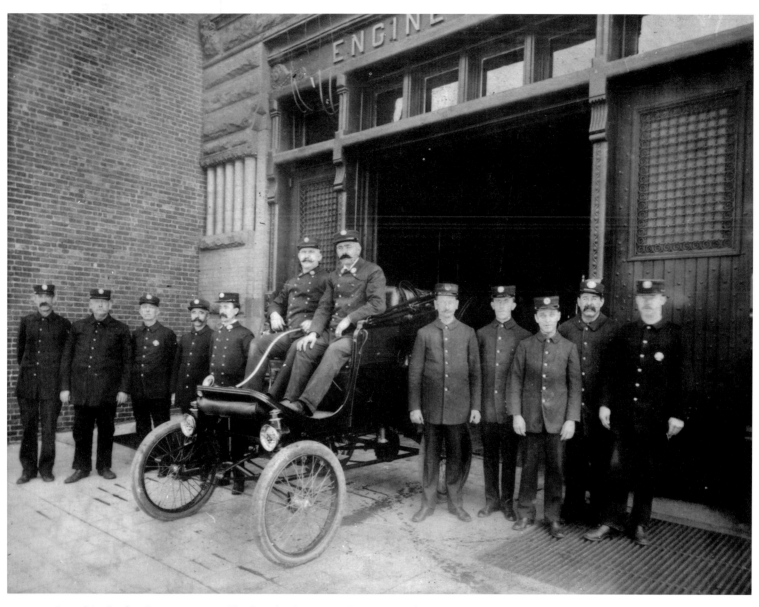

Seated in the fire department car, Chief Michael Dunn and Captain Arthur J. McMahon pose with uniformed members of Truck Company No. 1 (Engine Company No. 2) on Washington Street around 1908.

Hoboken's Lyric Theatre opened in 1886 and seated 1,800. Seen here in 1907, the venue hosted a variety of entertainers running the gamut from Lillie Langtry, to Burns and Allen, to Jack Benny. Located on Hudson Street, it closed in the mid- 1940s.

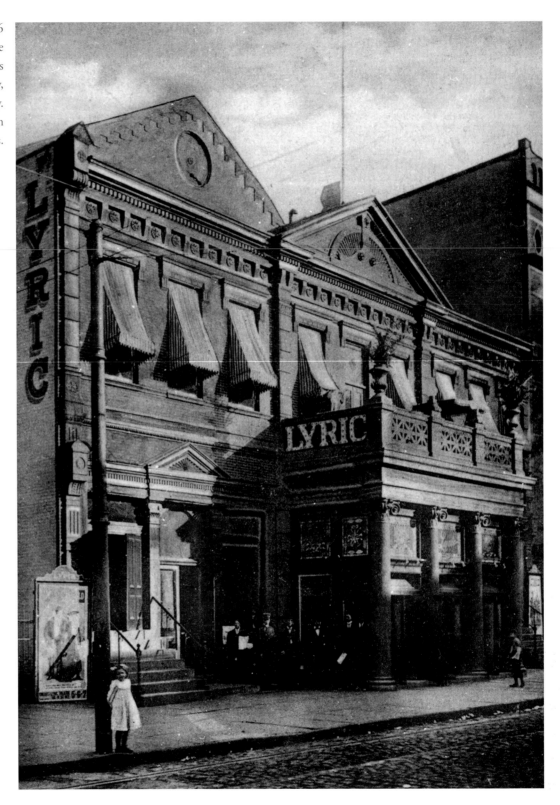

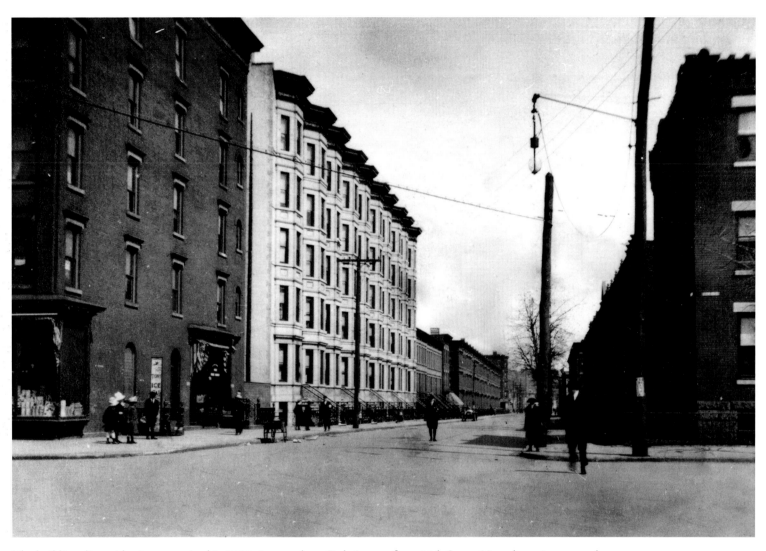

The buildings line wide city streets in this 1909 view north on Park Avenue from 11th Street. Note the unique street lamp.

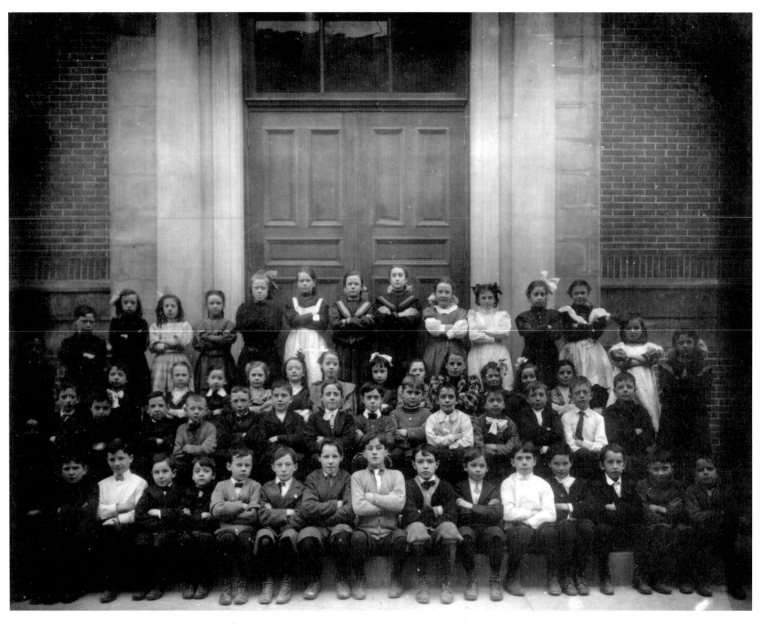

Pupils in the first and second grade at St. Joseph Parochial School at 79 Jackson Street pose for a group photo in 1909.

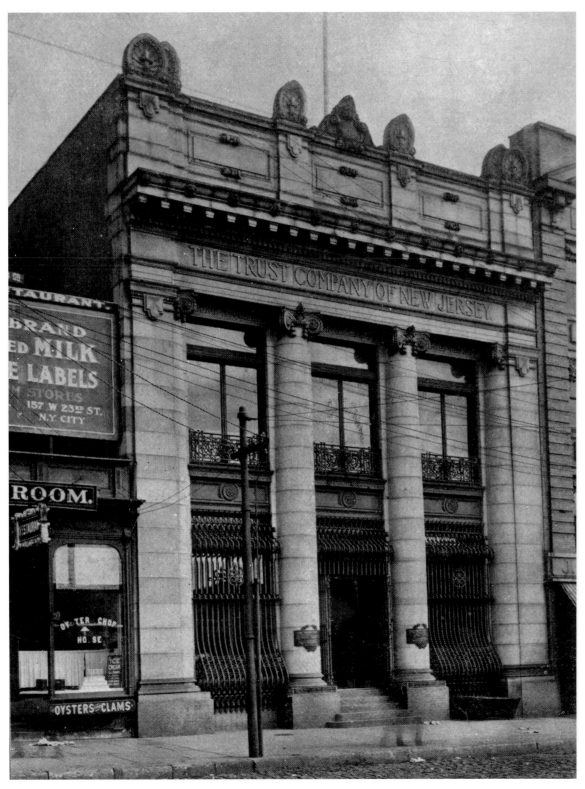

Chartered in 1899 and seen here a decade later, the Trust Company of New Jersey is located on Hudson Place. It was the fifth bank established in a city that used its geographic location to establish strong commercial ties.

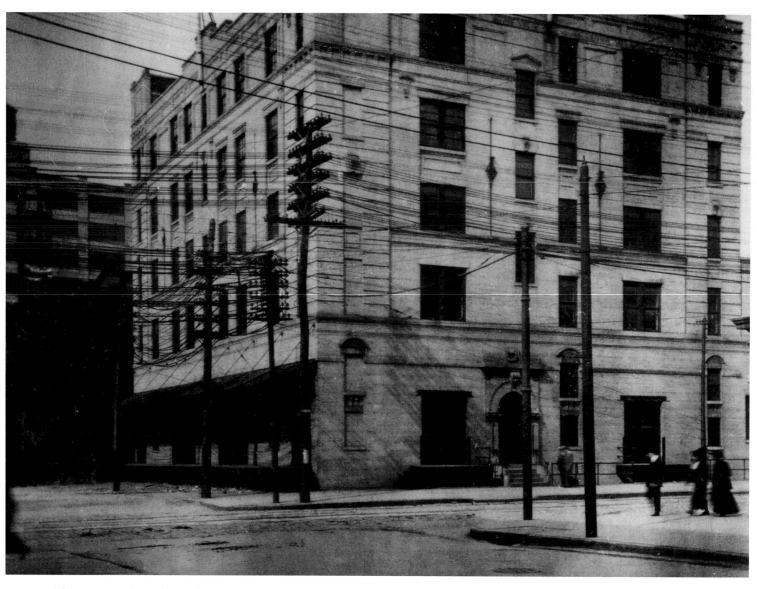

The American Grocer's warehouse on 14th Street, seen around 1910, was one of many such buildings used to store the variety of goods that moved in and out of Hoboken by ship and rail.

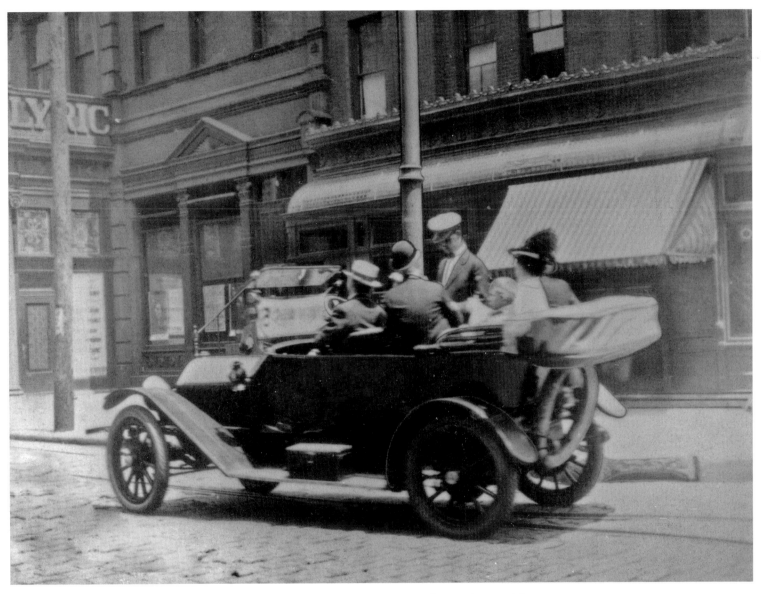

A jitney autobus on Washington Street in 1915 is perhaps taking its occupants to a show at the Lyric Theatre.

Following spread: A Civil War cannon stands in front of the Stevens House on the grounds of the Stevens Institute of Technology around 1915. The institute was established as a mechanical engineering school but eventually incorporated other courses of study. It fosters a research environment and maintains rigid standards today. Noted alumni include sculptor Alexander Calder, creator of the mobile, and Alfred Fielding, co-inventor of bubble wrap.

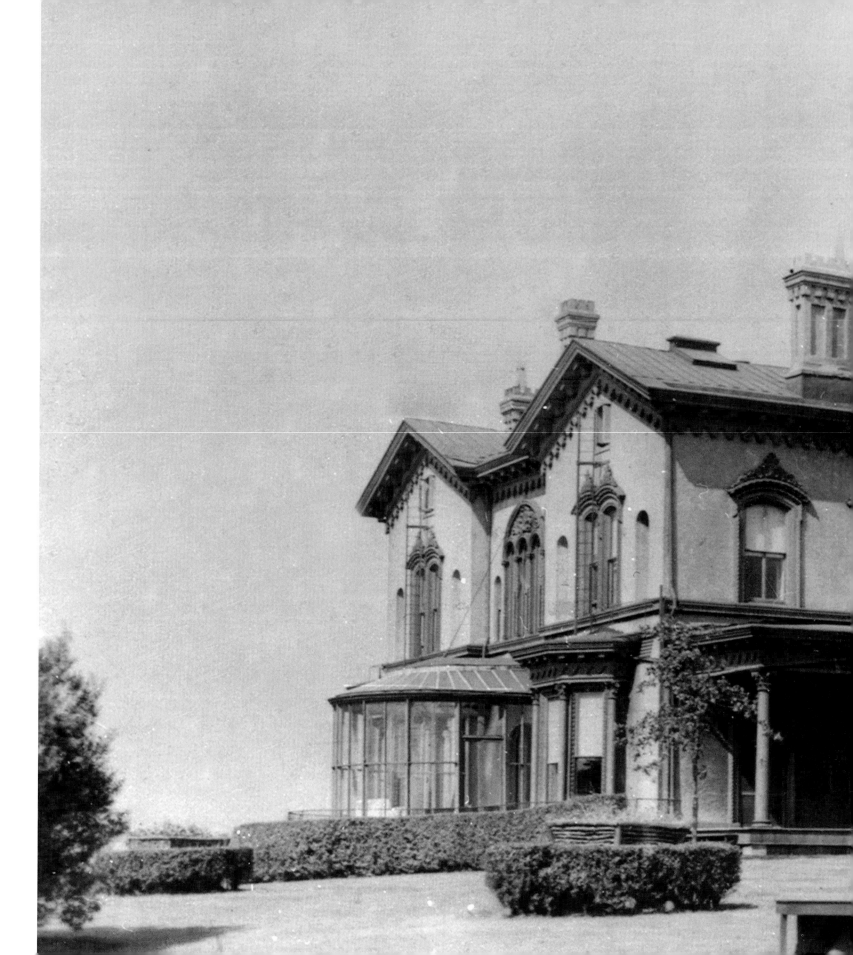

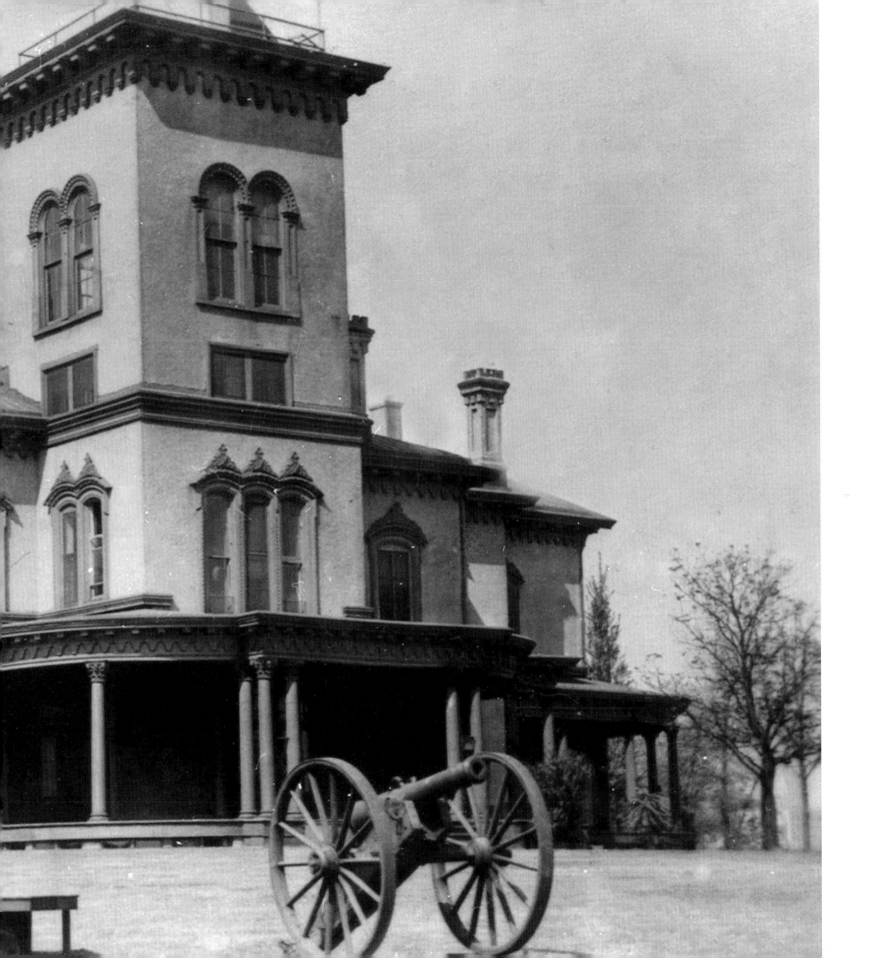

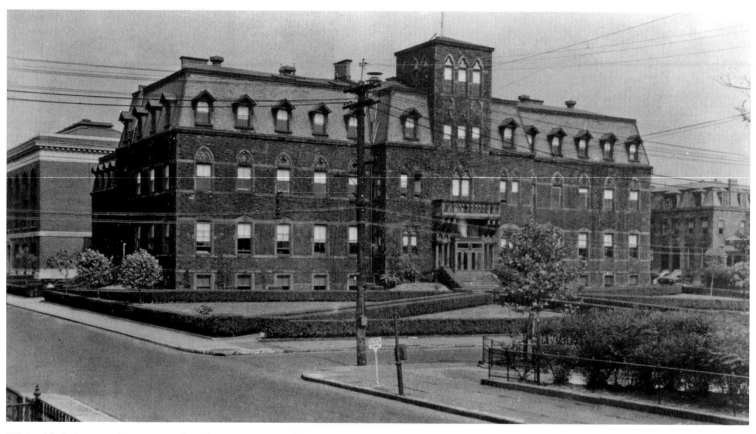

With added classes and programs, the Administration Building at Stevens Institute, seen here around 1916, would later change somewhat. The terrace would be removed, and the basement windows would be enlarged to accommodate modern machinery for the future engineers to work with.

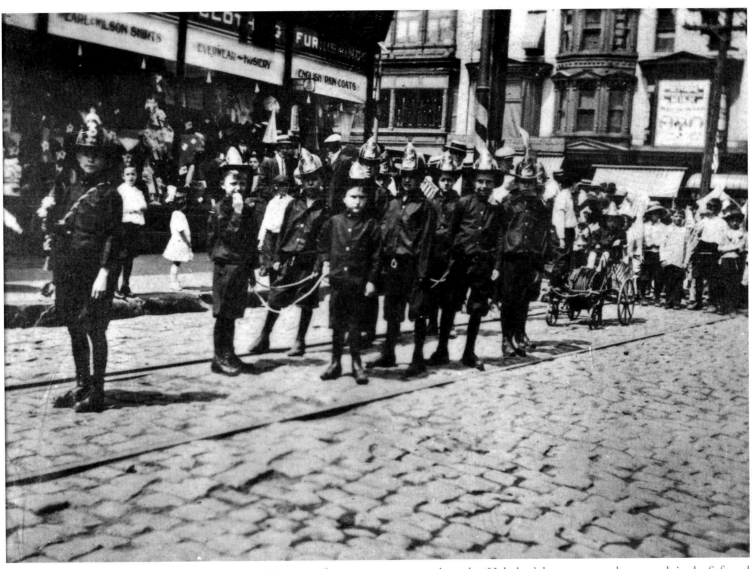

With very authentic-looking uniforms and their own fire wagon, youngsters dressed as Hoboken's bravest get ready to march in the Safe and Sane Parade around 1913.

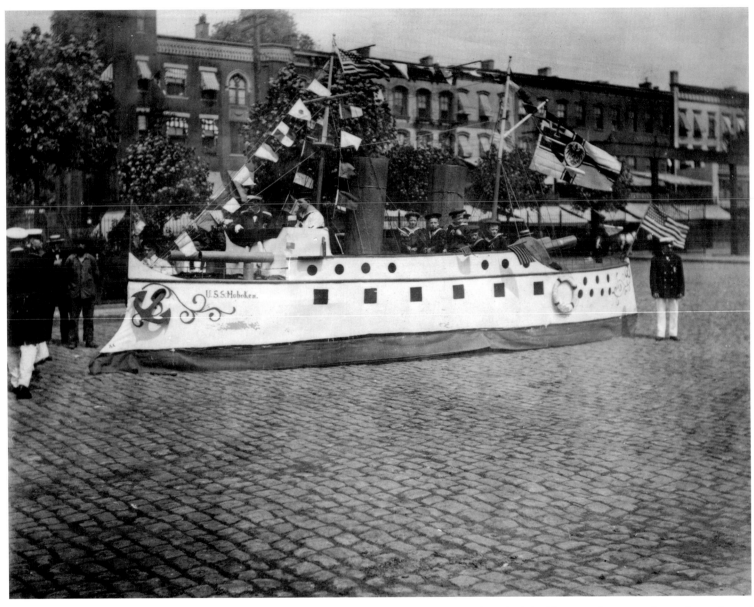

Safe and Sane Parades were started to promote more peaceful Fourth of July Parades, which had become dangerous due to fireworks and alcohol consumption. The 1913 Safe and Sane Parade included this model of the USS *Hoboken* presented by the North German Lloyd line and photographed on River Street. It was decorated with American and German Imperial flags.

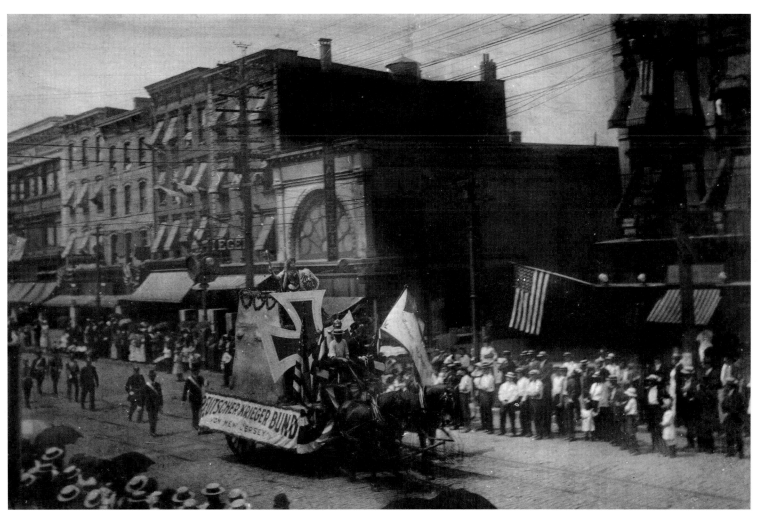

The 1913 Safe and Sane Parade also featured this German "Bund Von New Jersey" horse-drawn float.

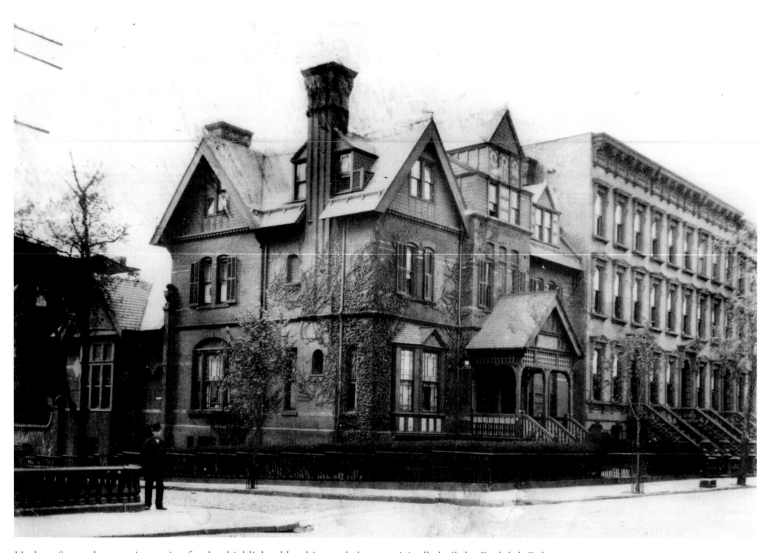

Hudson Street shows quite a mix of styles, highlighted by this stately house originally built by Rudolph Rabe.

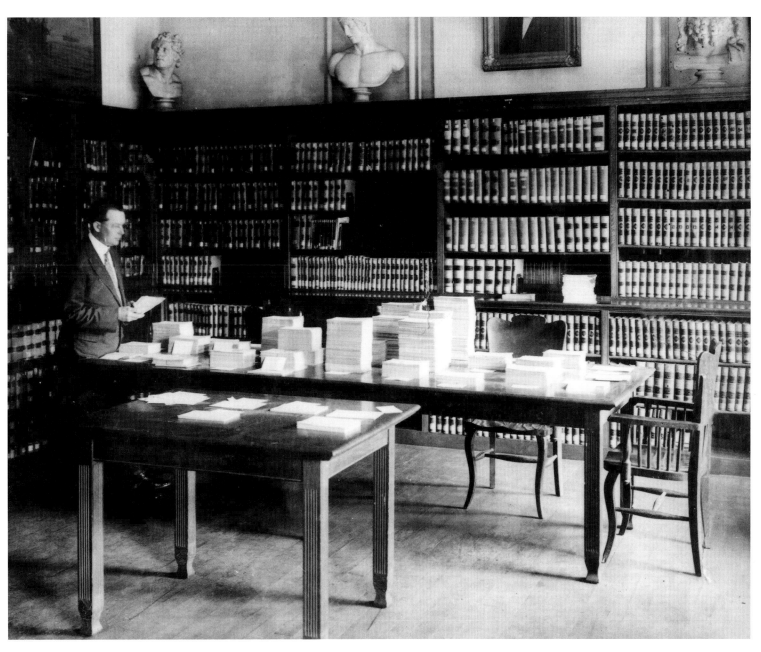

Edward Russ surveys the collection of law books he generously donated to the Hoboken Public Library. The Russ Law Library opened officially in September 1912.

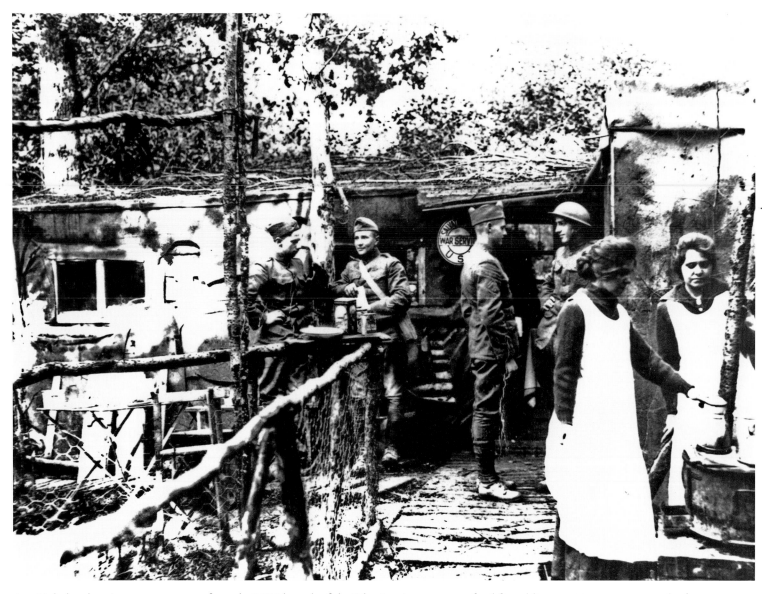

At a Hoboken location, young women from the USO branch of the Salvation Army prepare food for soldiers awaiting transport to the front during World War I.

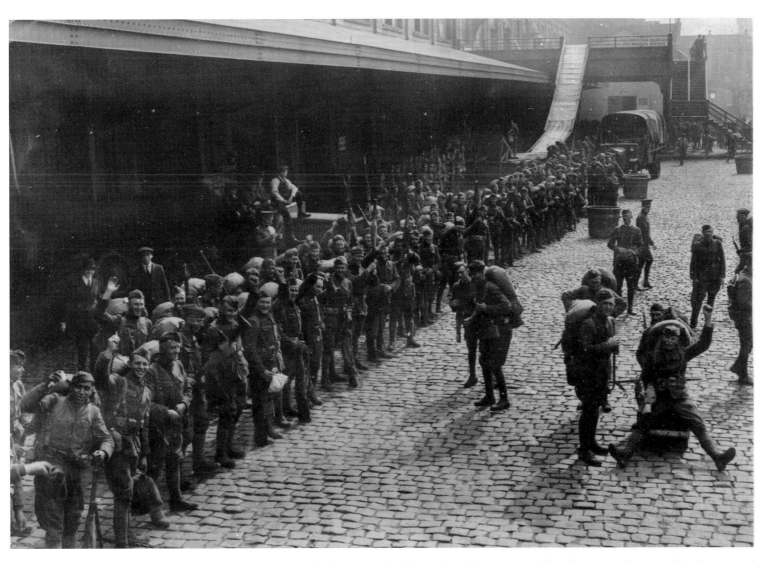

Doughboys at a Hoboken pier are lined up for embarkation on the SS *President Grant* in 1917. The *Grant* was a German ship that moored in a neutral port when World War I began. It was subsequently seized and used for troop transport. She served the military in World War II as well.

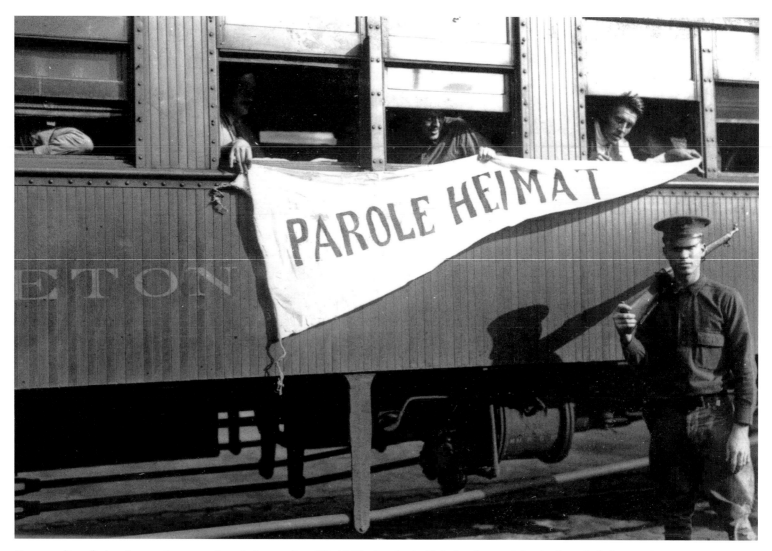

German aliens facing deportation upon America's entry into World War I arrive in Hoboken by special train from Oglethorpe, Georgia. Over 1,400 German nationals were transported on three trains. The "Parole Heimat" banner is loosely translated "Passport (or destination) Home."

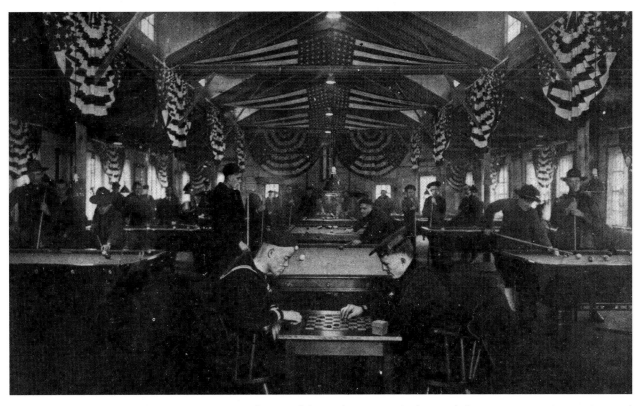

The billiard room seen here in 1918 was one feature of the Hudson Hut, which provided services to men in transit to and from Europe. The facility served hundreds of soldiers and sailors in Hoboken and remained open until 1919.

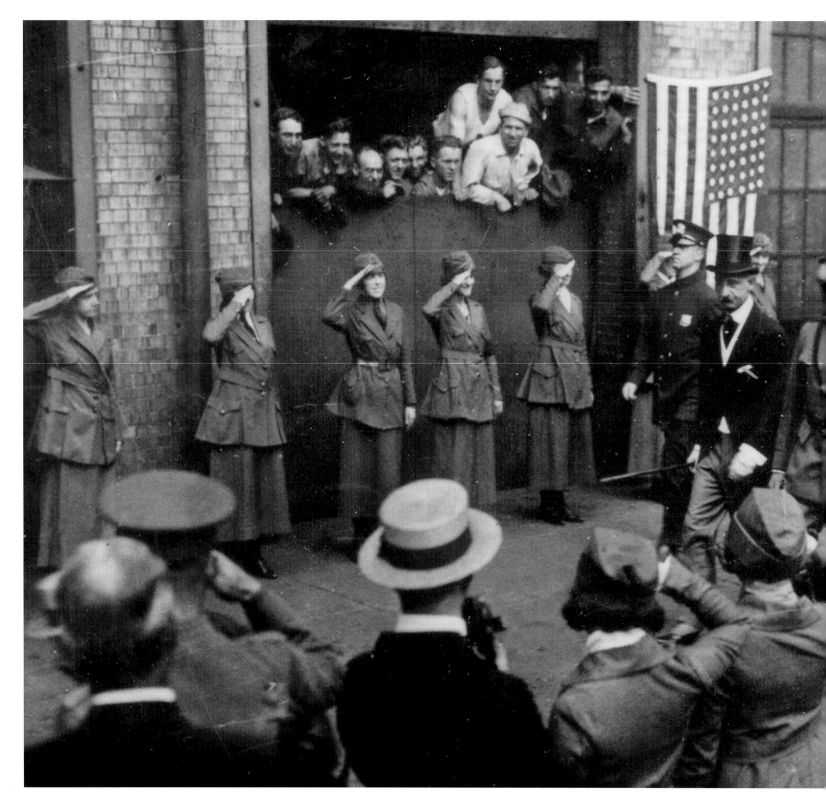

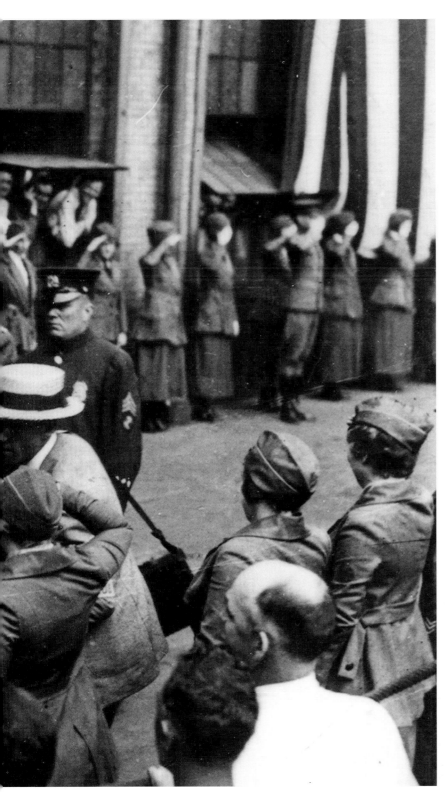

Transport service personnel salute General John J. "Black Jack" Pershing on Hoboken's Pier 4 in 1919. Accompanying Pershing is Rodman Wanamaker, in the top hat, famous department store heir and a booster of American aviation.

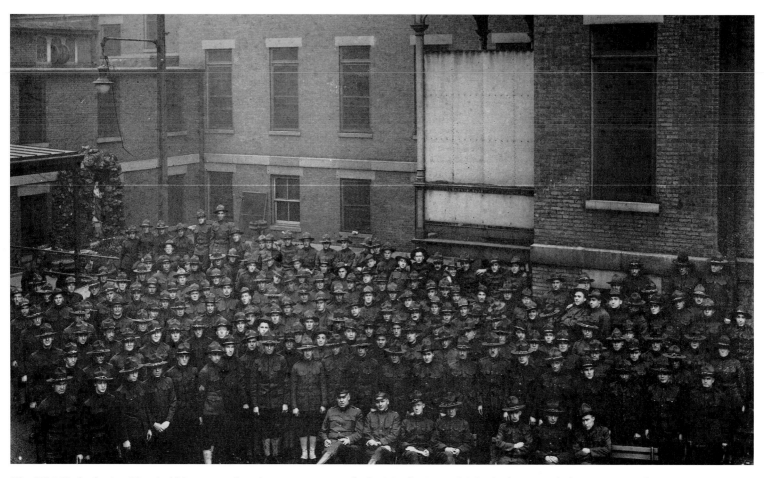

The USA Embarkation Hospital No. 1, seen here in 1917, was actually St. Mary's Hospital. The facility provided cantonments for men going to Europe or for wounded coming home, and could care for more than 700.

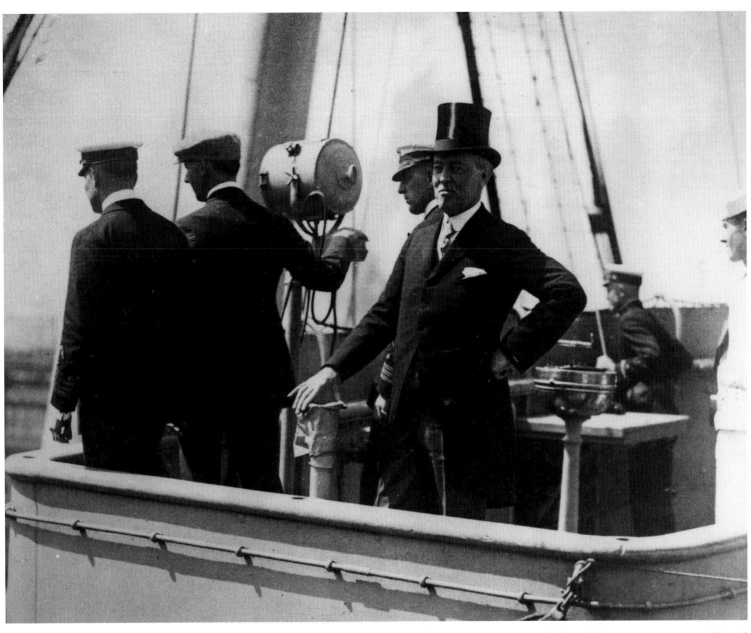

President Woodrow Wilson stands on the deck of the USS *George Washington* as it arrives at Hoboken, July 8, 1919—a true presidential pose for a former governor of New Jersey. He was returning from the post–World War I peace conference in France.

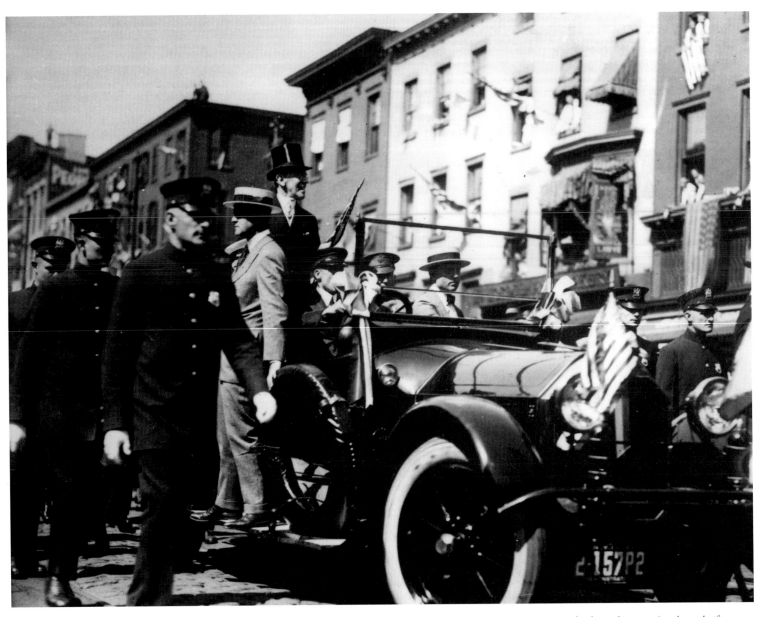

A motorcade carries President Wilson down Washington Street on July 8, 1919. Note the secret service agent perched on the running board of the president's car.

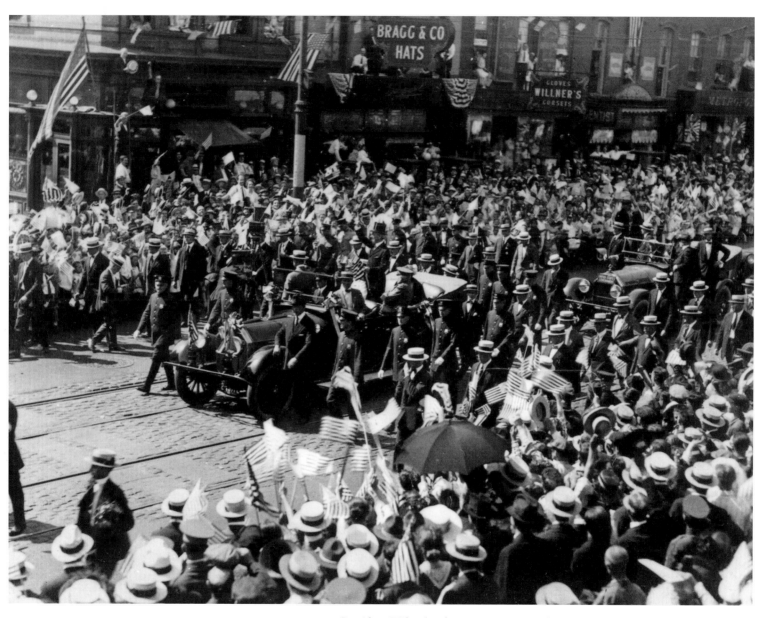

President Wilson's July 8, 1919, motorcade passes the Bragg & Company hat shop.

Four Girl Scouts pose in costume in the 1920s. The photo was taken in Columbus Park. A large pond and stone pavilion can be seen at side and behind, respectively.

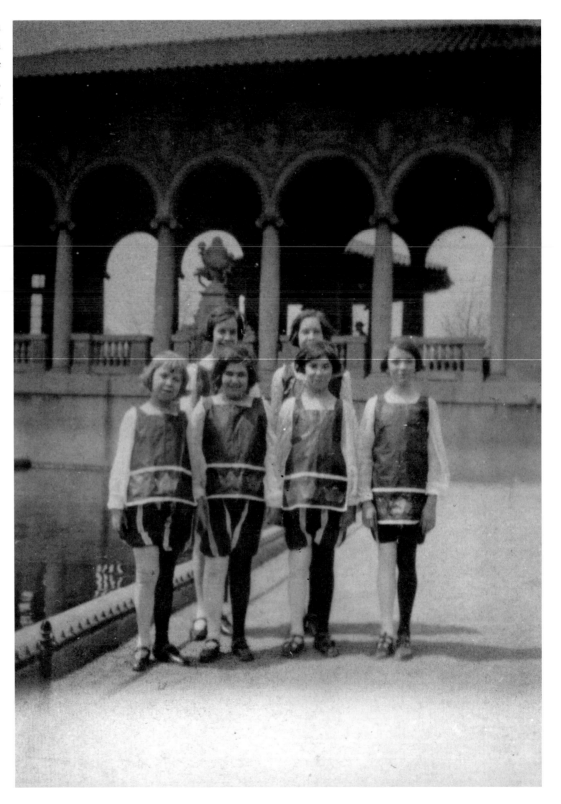

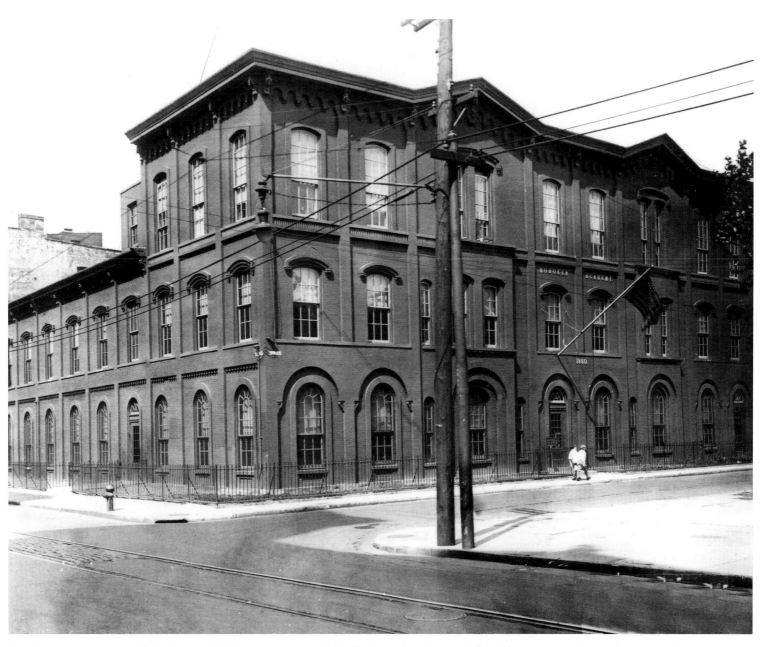

On the northeast corner of 5th Street and Willow Avenue stood the Hoboken Academy, established in 1861 as a German language and culture school. It is believed to have housed the first kindergarten in the United States. Merging with Stevens Prep in 1934, it became Stevens Academy in 1950 and closed in 1974. The building was demolished to make way for a bank.

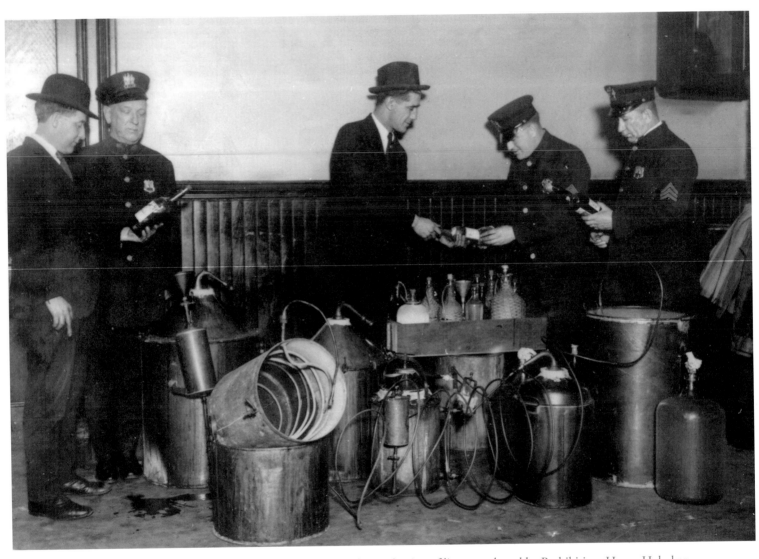

The Roaring Twenties brought increased illegal activity, especially in the production of liquor outlawed by Prohibition. Here a Hoboken raid has resulted in confiscation of paraphernalia for making "bathtub gin." Added vigilance may have stemmed from a January 1921 incident in which six residents died from wood-alcohol poisoning.

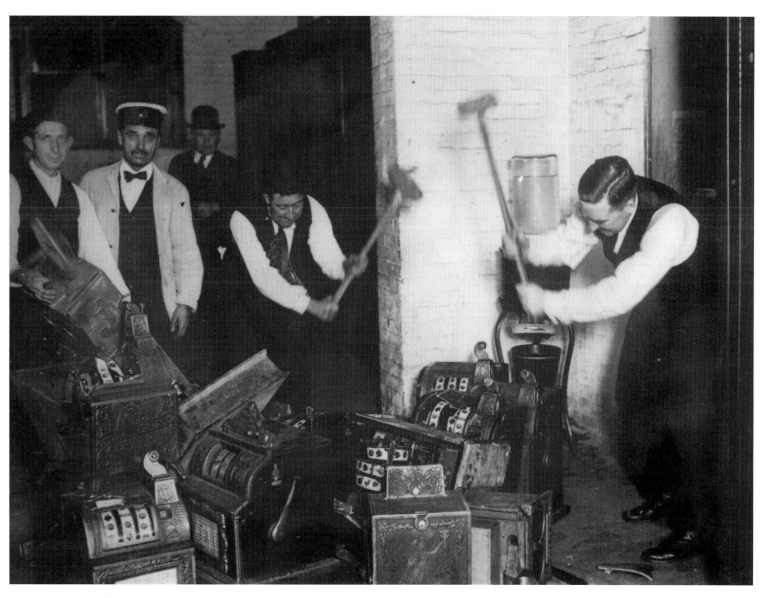

In the 1920s social vices were not confined to the imbibing of alcoholic beverages, though some would say liquor went arm in arm with the illegal "one-armed bandits." Here Hoboken detectives take sledgehammers to confiscated gambling equipment.

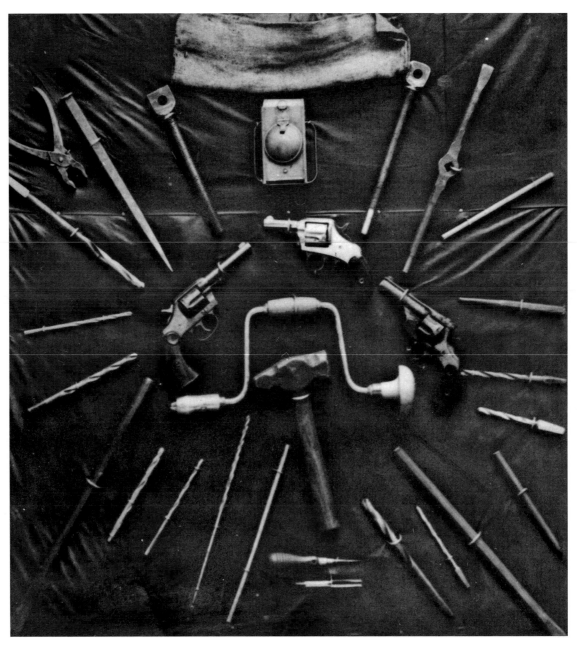

An active police department will build interesting evidence collections. These weapons and burglar's tools seized by the Hoboken police include drills, jimmies, a hammer, and three pistols.

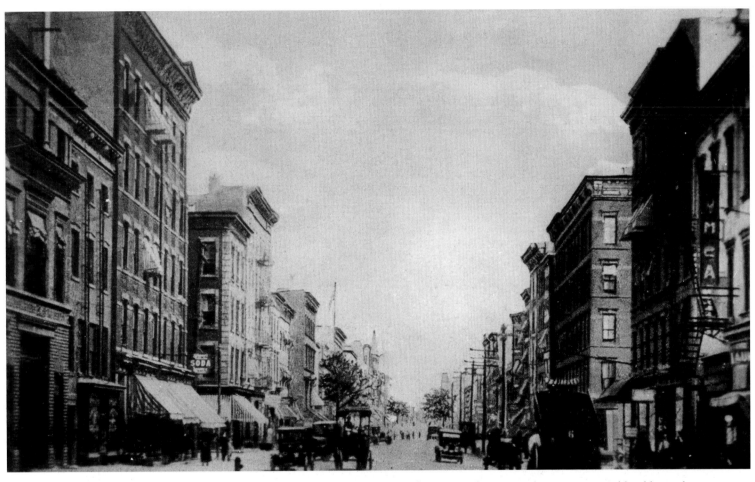

In this mid-1920s view of Hudson Street near 2nd Street, a variety of commercial stores can be seen at ground level beneath apartments. The Fire Department's headquarters is at left and a YMCA building at right.

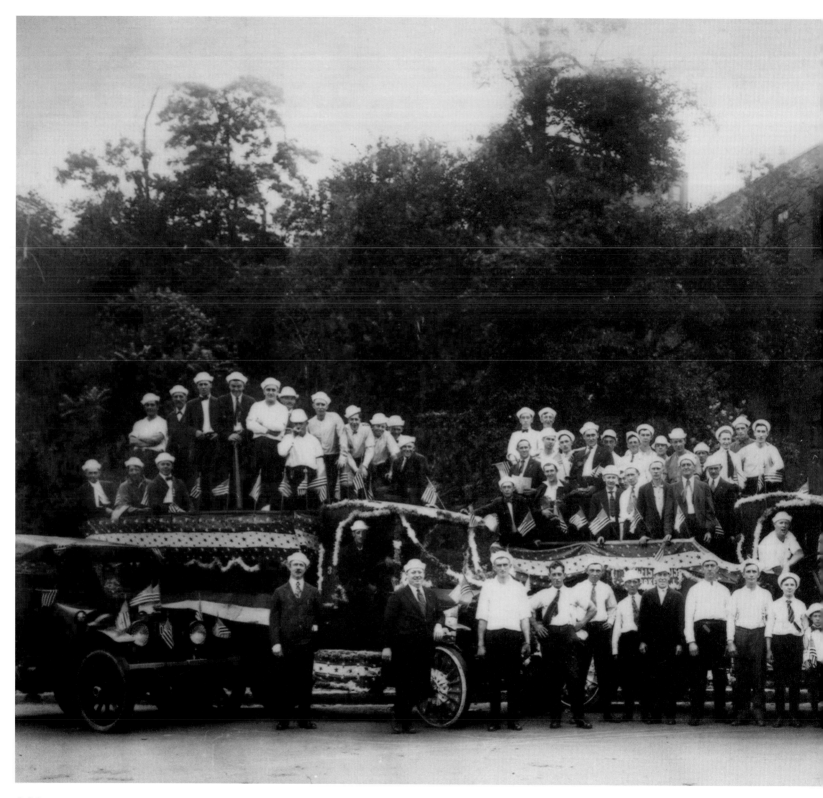

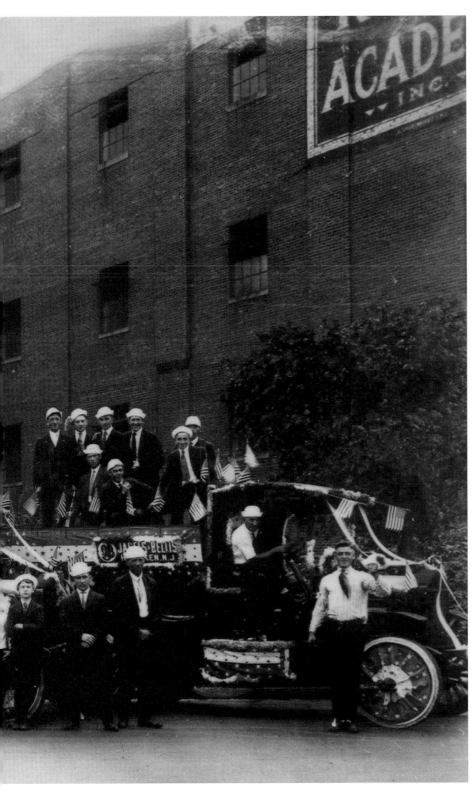

Workers and families from the Jagels-Bellis Coal Company pose on three flatbed trucks in preparation for a Hoboken parade in 1920. With its wide thoroughfares, Hoboken loved and still loves a parade. The coal business was lucrative in the city. Coal stoves were in Hoboken homes, and coal boilers powered shipping.

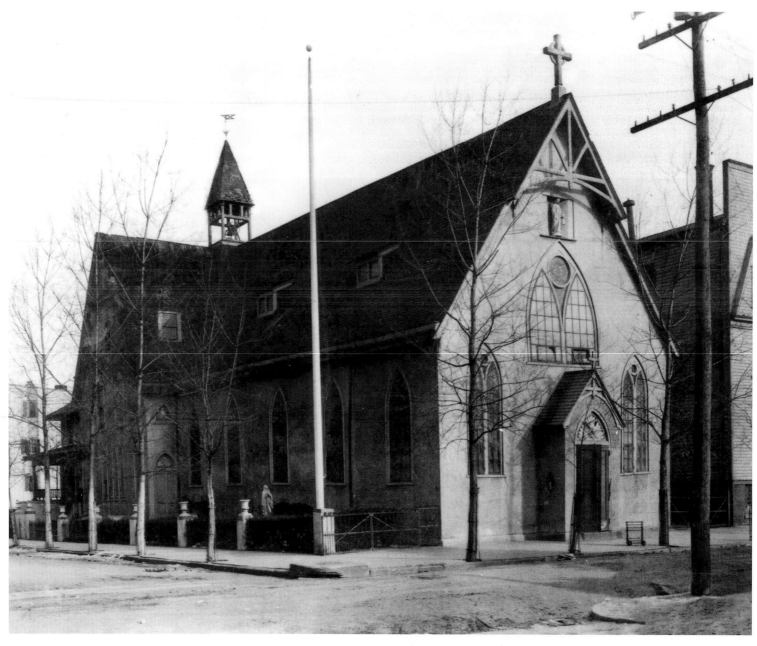

The Church of St. Ann is located at Jefferson and 7th streets. Italian Catholics of the area who had been meeting in a basement at 4th and Jefferson moved to a storefront right after the turn of the century. Masses were said in a makeshift chapel. As the congregation grew, plans for a church materialized and this *Parochia di S. Anna* opened in 1906. St. Ann's feast day is July 26th, so a *festa,* or celebration, was instituted that carries on to this day, though the church has since moved.

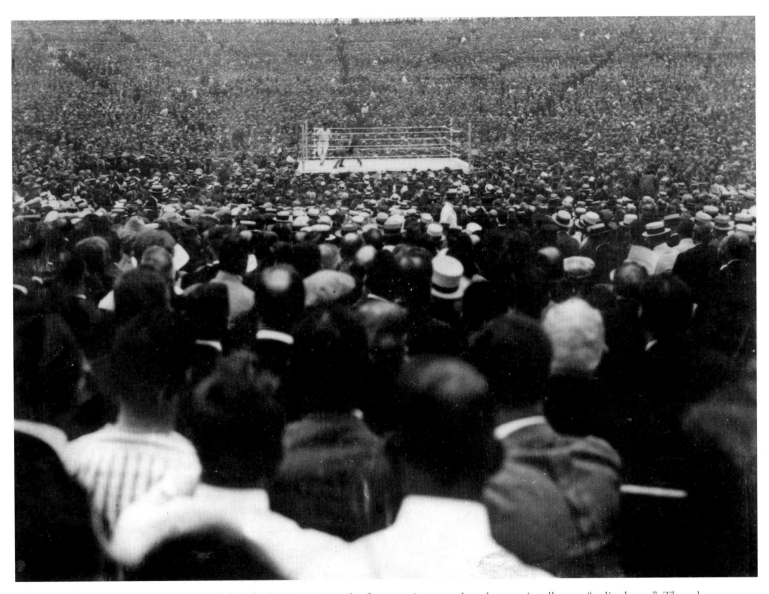

The Jack Dempsey–Georges Carpentier fight of July 2, 1921, was the first sporting event broadcast nationally over "radiophone." Though the fight took place in Jersey City, Hoboken radio station WJY broadcast it to 61 cities. From ringside, J. Andrew White spoke by phone to J. O. Smith at the Hoboken location. A 400-foot tower was installed atop Lackawanna Terminal. Monies made at the reception sites were donated to the American Committee for a Devastated France. Carpentier was the French champion. Dempsey won in a fourth-round knockout.

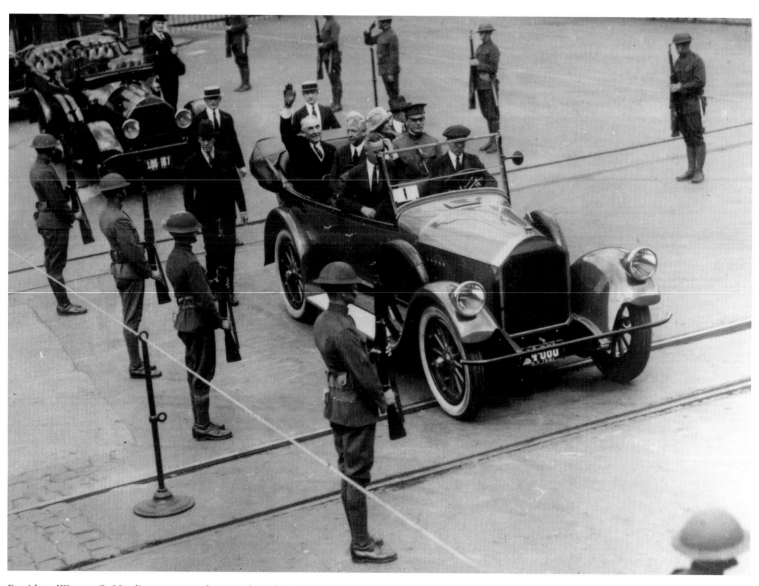

President Warren G. Harding waves to the crowd on the Army Piers on May 24, 1921. Services were being held for the 5,212 war dead being returned from military cemeteries in France aboard the transport ship *Wheaton*. Representatives from all states in the Union as well as a multitude of European officials attended.

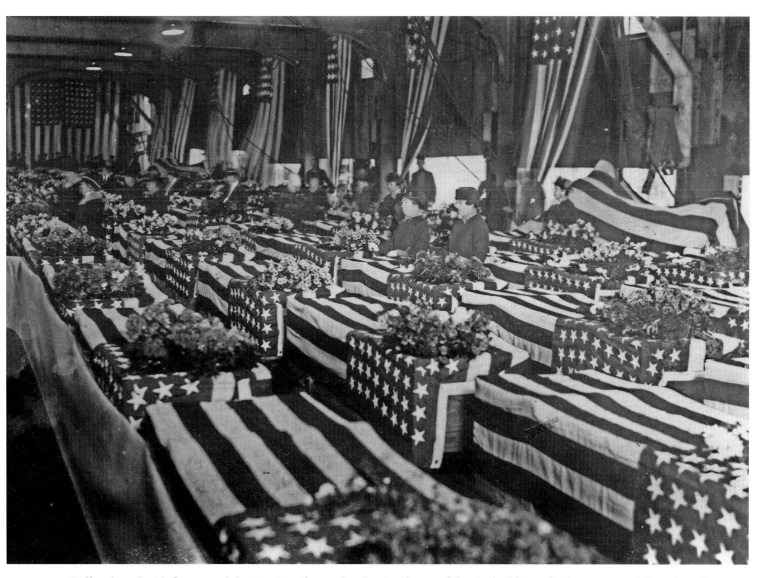

Coffins draped with flowers and the American flag are lined up inside one of the pier buildings after being removed from the *Wheaton* on May 24, 1921. Women of the Hoboken War Mothers are placing the bouquets.

At a Hoboken ceremony of July 10, 1921, General Pershing, Commander of the American Expeditionary Forces in World War I, and Senator Henry Cabot Lodge are among those present to honor the first three American soldiers who died in France.

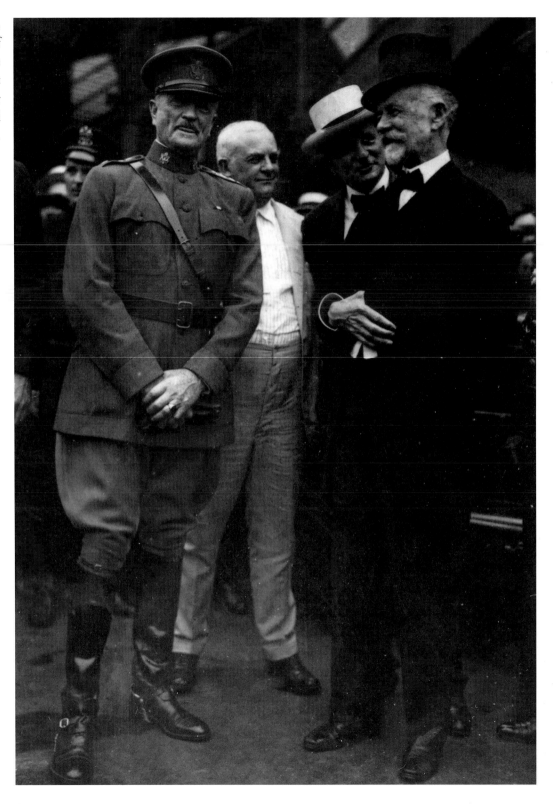

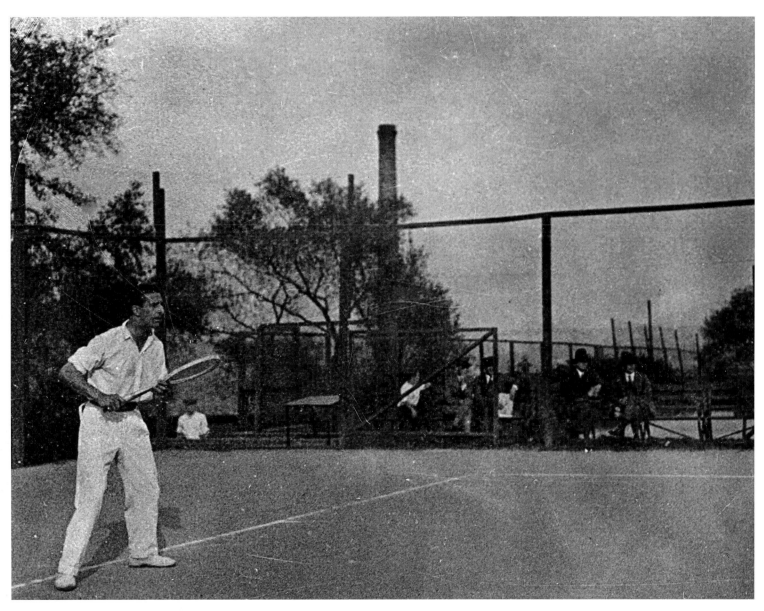

Manuel Alonzo, the Spanish tennis champion, works out in the early 1920s at the Hoboken Tennis Club. This image shows the blend of activities that can exist in a hardworking city. The court is only a short distance away from an industrial smokestack. The Hoboken Tennis Club is still active and thriving.

Flags adorn the apartments and storefronts of Washington Street during the 1922 Decoration Day Parade. Girl Scouts march past Solomon's Suits and Wearbest Clothes. Decoration Day is now Memorial Day.

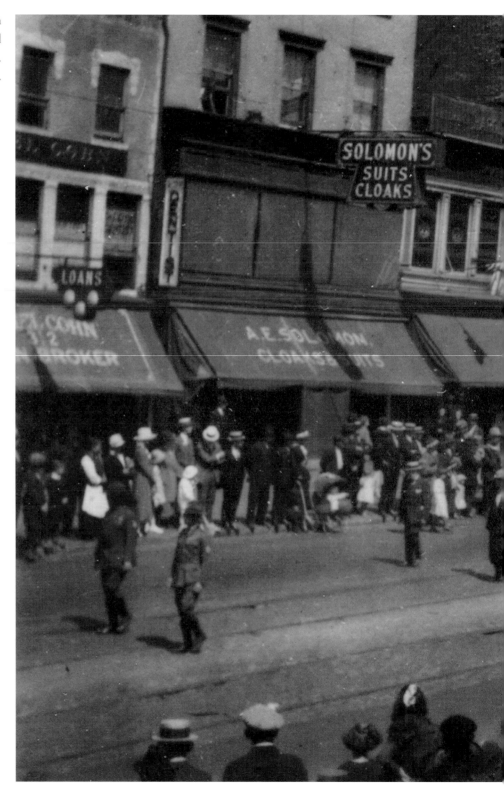

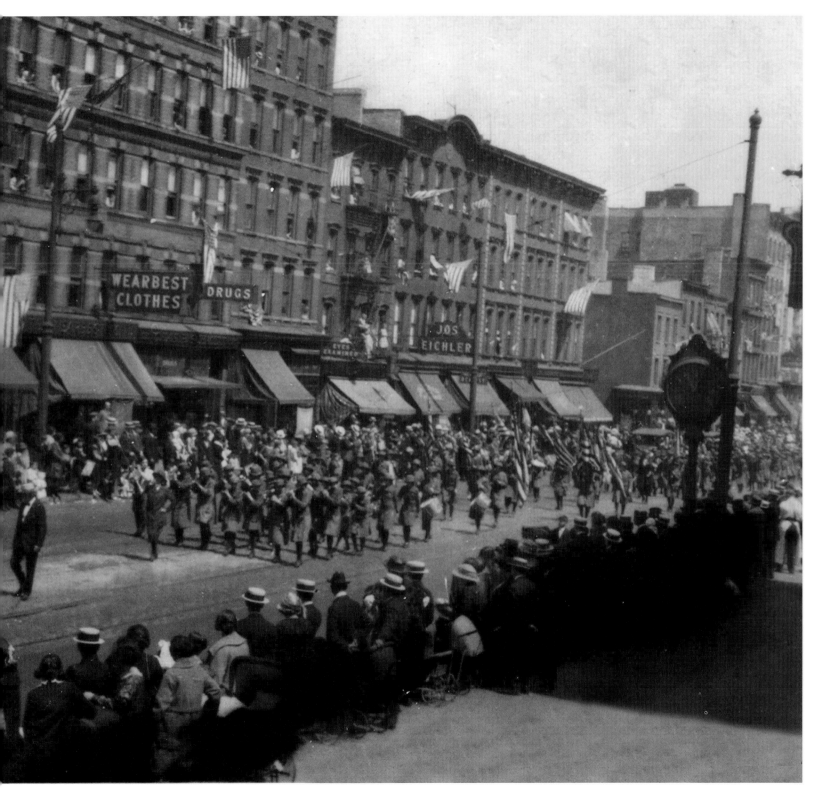

The Hofbrau Haus restaurant and Central Hotel occupy the corner of River and 2nd streets here in the late 1920s. The street-level eatery had booths and tables inside and a bandstand outside during summer. The business in 1925 had 10,000 capital shares outstanding, so it must have been a profitable undertaking.

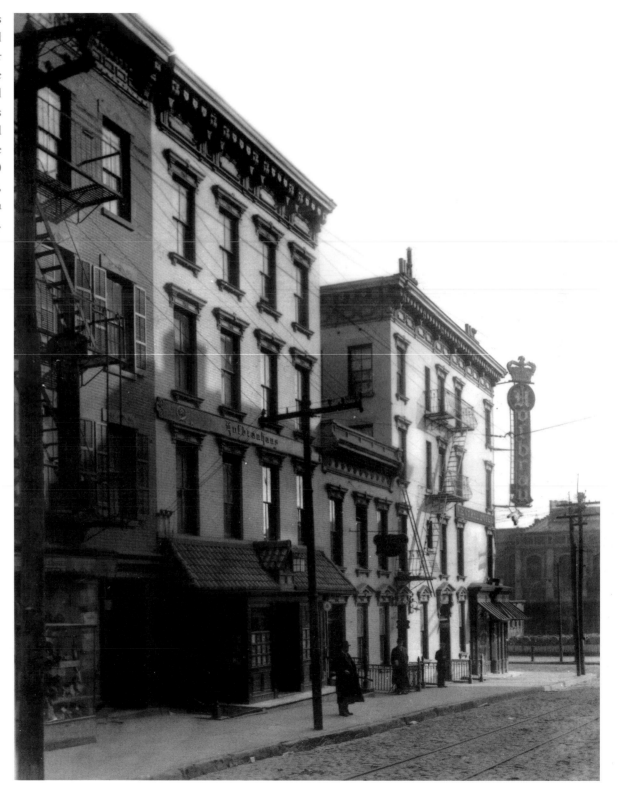

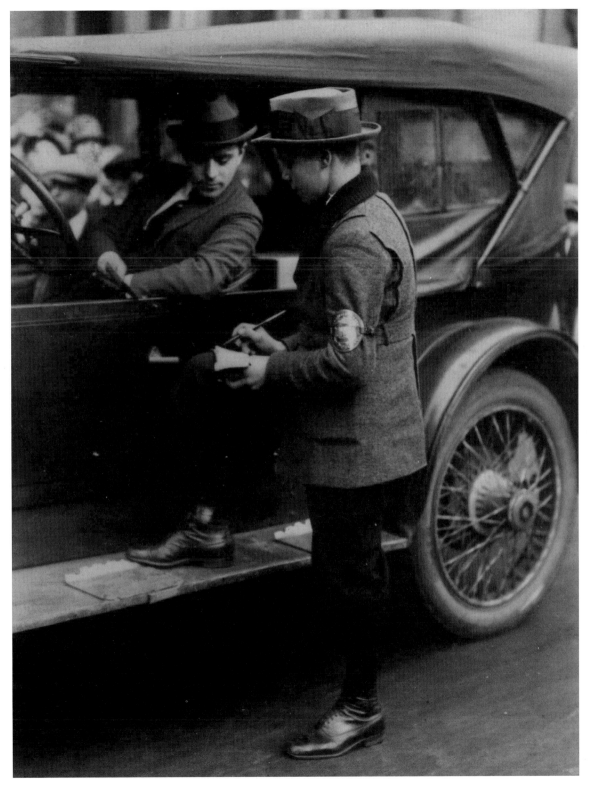

The Hoboken Police Department had a Junior Police corps staffed by teenagers. Here in 1923 one of the "patrol boys" strikes an official policemanlike pose, his foot on a car's running board while giving a summons to the driver.

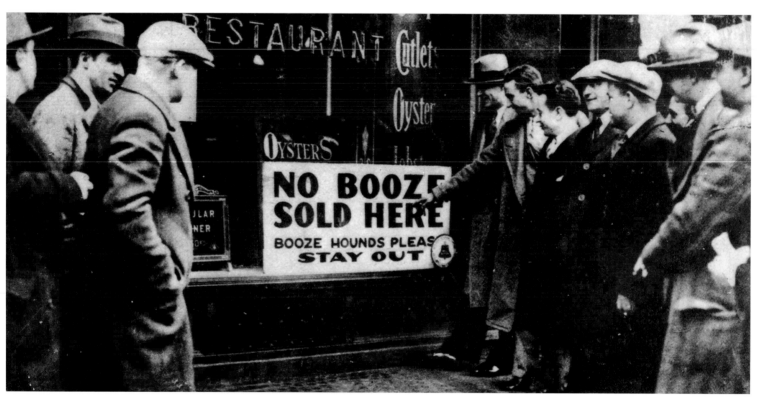

By 1929, Prohibition had nearly run its course. In a town like Hoboken, which was once advertised as having a bar on every corner, speakeasies flourished. It got to the point where restaurant owner George Gonzales had to advertise—along with promoting his cutlets and oysters—that "booze hounds" should take their business elsewhere.

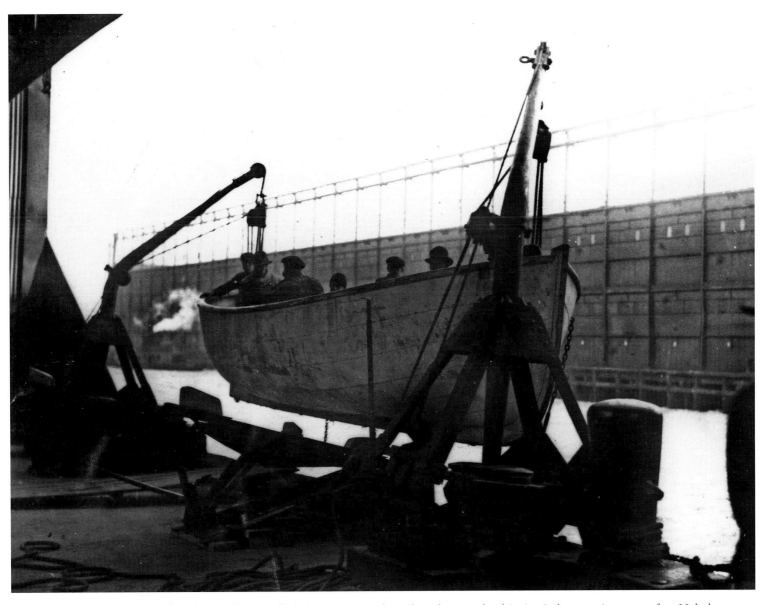

In the wake of the *Titanic* disaster of 1912, pressure was brought to bear on the shipping industry to improve safety. Hoboken was a maritime city, and various devices intended to make shipping safer were tested in its shipyards. Here lifeboat designs and equipment are being tested in January 1921.

After World War I, the drive to replace horse cavalry with mechanized equipment was underway. Here in December 1920 near Hoboken's Hudson Ice Company, military officials and a large group of onlookers scrutinize a "new type" 155-millimeter rifle mounted on a caterpillar track vehicle.

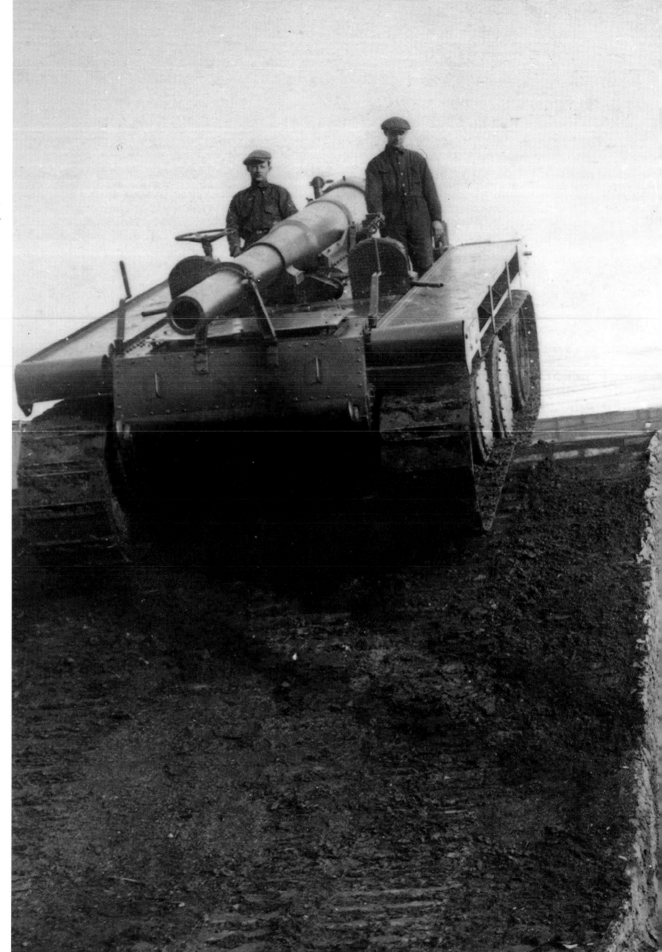

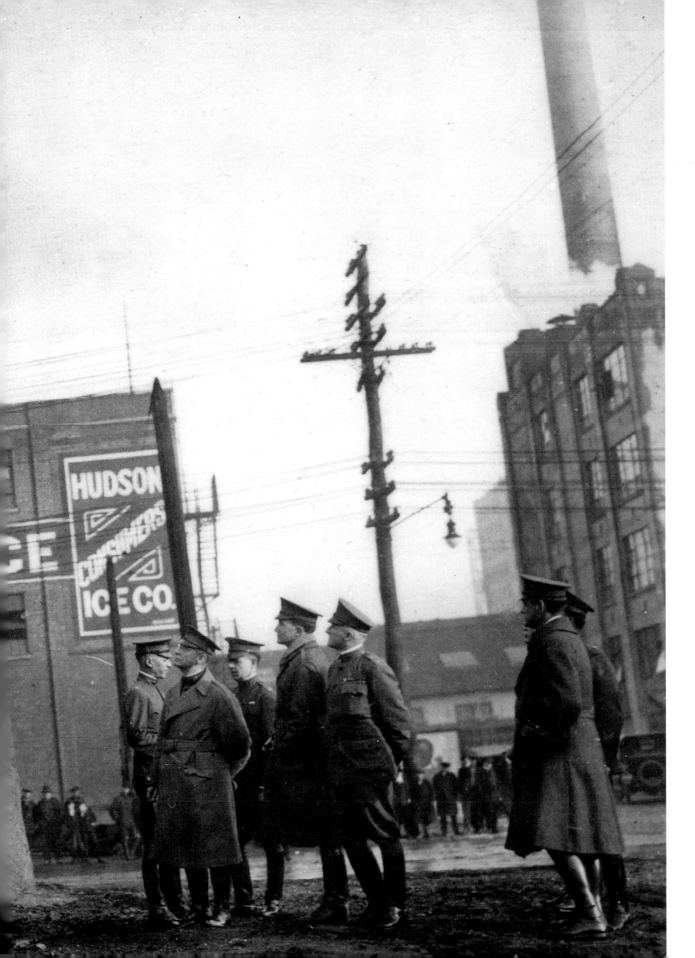

In this close-up view, a man demonstrates machinery used to lower what was billed as a nonsinkable lifeboat in January 1921.

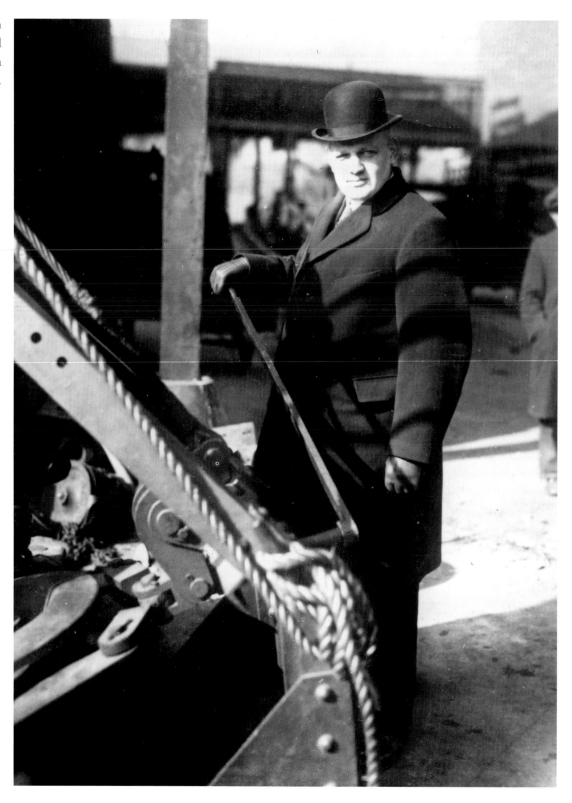

OFF AND ON THE WATERFRONT

(1930–1979)

During World War II, Hoboken was a vital shipbuilding center. Most of the ships were smaller auxiliary craft but important to the war effort nonetheless. There were ample opportunities for Rosie the Riveter. War materials were also manufactured in the city.

After the war, the economy remained stable. The city had strong ethnic, religious, and family ties. The soldiers who were returning and taking advantage of the GI Bill stayed for a time. Shipbuilding was still viable, and Maxwell House Coffee and Lipton Tea kept a presence in the city. The Port Authority of New York and New Jersey, created in 1921, maintained the port facilities while managing the rail, ferry, bridges, tunnels, and other transportation services. *On the Waterfront,* starring Marlon Brando, was filmed in the city in 1953-54. Frank Sinatra was still on top, and Hoboken was still an upbeat city.

As was the case in many places, Hoboken changed in the 1960s. The shipping industry looked for cheaper labor elsewhere. The Port Authority shifted commerce to newer facilities on the Newark Bay. People became tired of the urban environment, and the suburbs beckoned. Cities began to look dingy, Hoboken among them.

Hoboken was in a cocoon through the 1970s and even into the 1980s. Then someone looked at Hoboken as Hudson must have done. Land speculators eyeing the shore realized such waterfront communities could be vital arteries for a new community of urban dwellers. The city began to blossom anew. Buildings like Keuffel & Esser were converted to artist lofts and apartments. Old warehouses were torn down to be replaced by condominiums. Thankfully, the Hoboken Terminal was saved and designated a historic landmark. The architecture that gave Hoboken its charm was recognized, and the city is now a mix of old and new. It maintains a financial base closely linked to New York City. It again includes people of many nationalities, and new and old cultures are celebrated. Hoboken is a success story. How can you tell? Try and find a parking space.

Seen here in the 1930s, Our Lady of Grace Orphanage on Willow Avenue between 4th and 5th streets was associated with Our Lady of Grace Church.

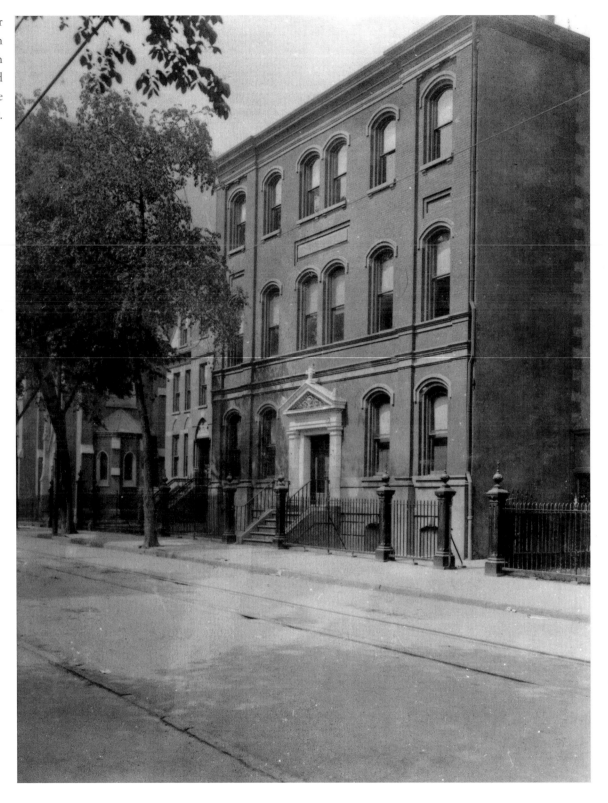

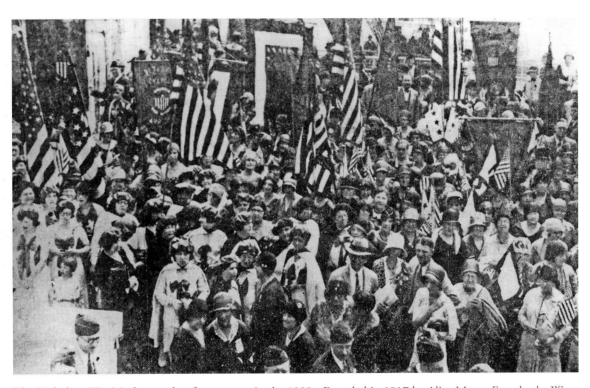

The Hoboken War Mothers gather for an event in the 1930s. Founded in 1917 by Alice Moore French, the War Mothers did much patriotic work. It was an organization for mothers of servicemen who had served or were serving in the armed forces. The Hoboken chapter must have taken on an added burden since the sons of so many mothers from around the country embarked for Europe from the New Jersey city.

Following spread: The tables outside Meyers Hotel provide a true sidewalk-cafe feel. The hotel was built by Herman L. Timken, a prominent citizen of Hoboken who was elected mayor in 1883. The menu featured the standard German fare of Wiener schnitzel, pigs' knuckles, sauerbraten, and various wursts.

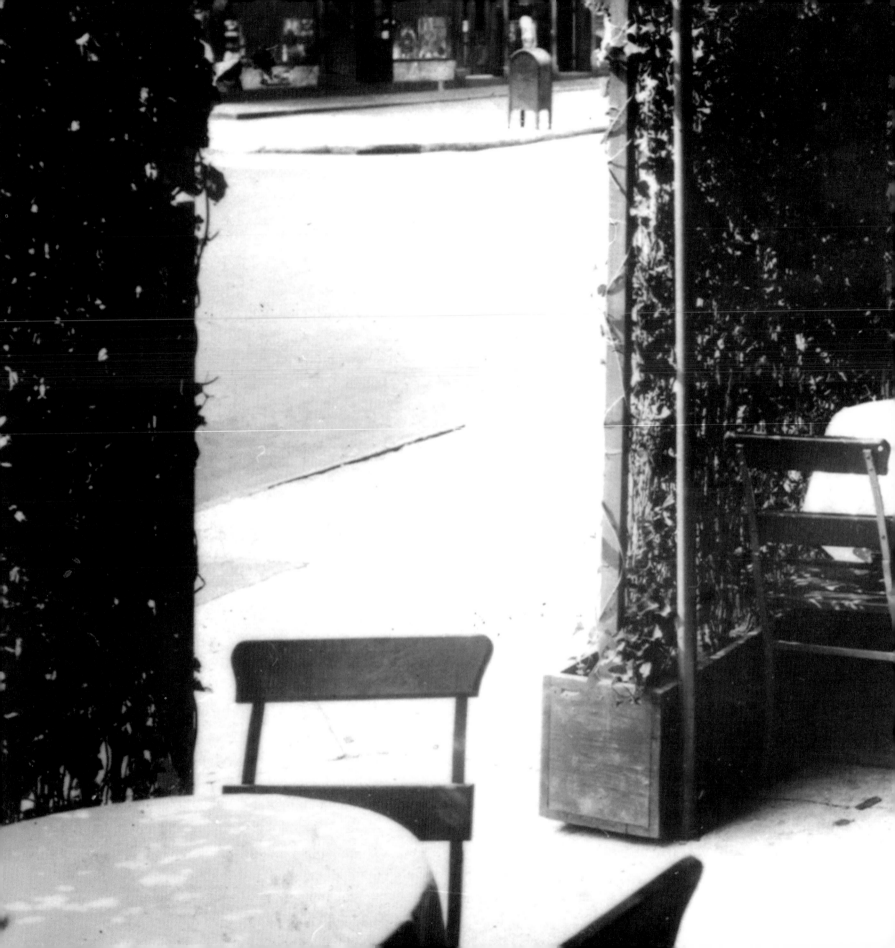

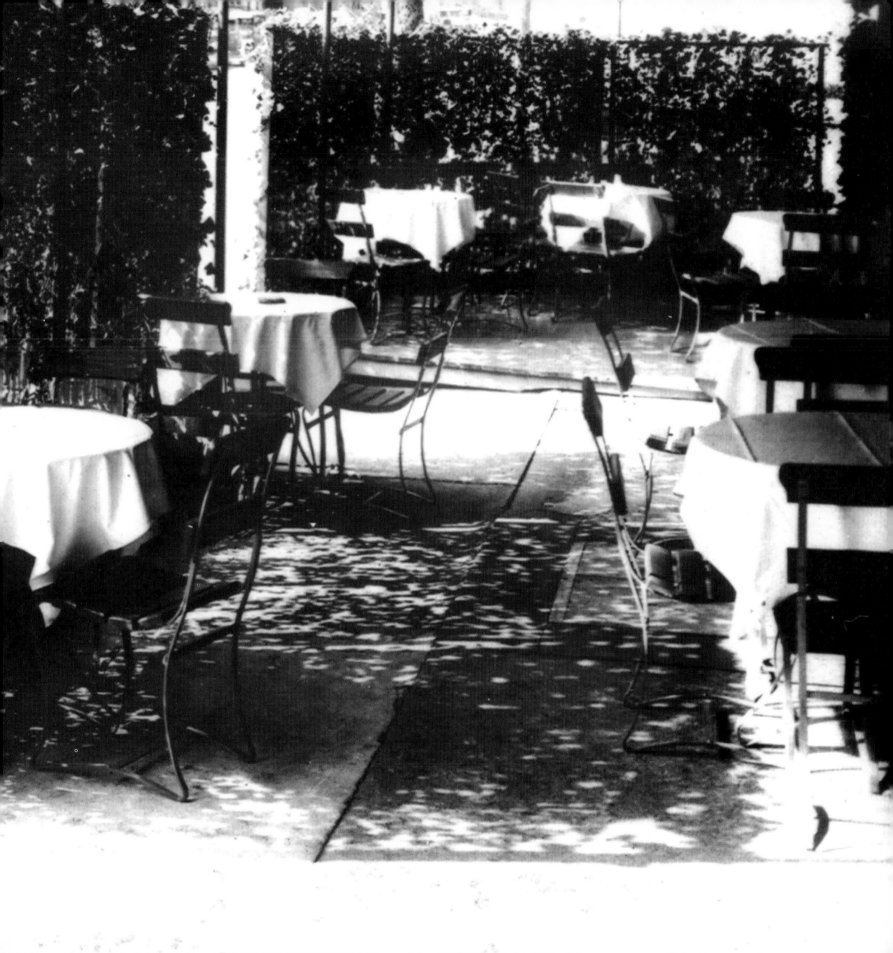

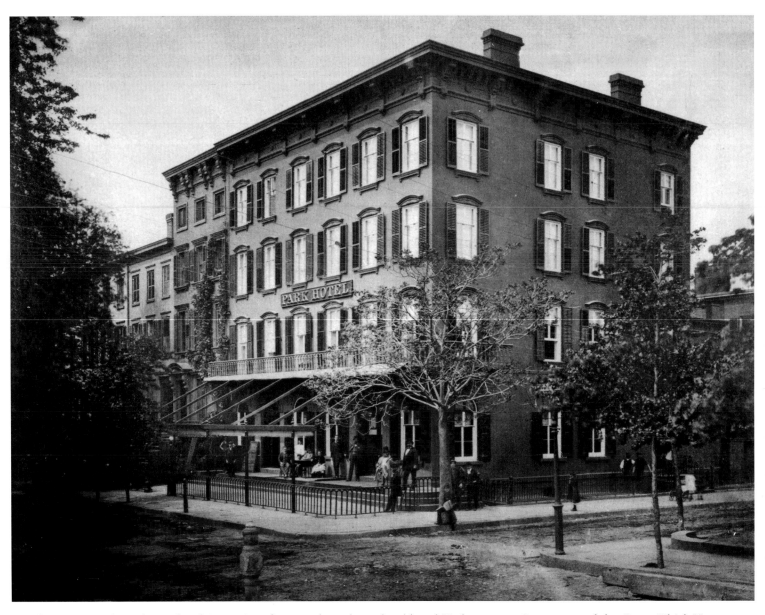

Seen here in 1933, the Park Hotel with its spacious front porch was located at 4th and Hudson streets. It was reported that Baron Ulrich Von Puttkamer, Bismarck's nephew, caused quite a stir when he lodged at the hotel after having left the Prussian Army following a dispute with one of his commanders in 1885.

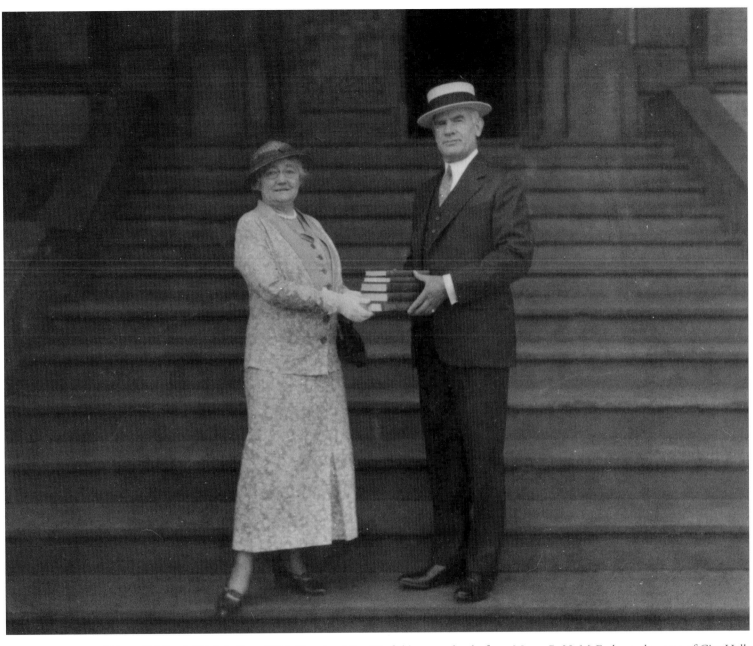

During Citizen Gift Book Week in June 1936, librarian Nina Hatfield accepts books from Mayor B. N. McFeely on the steps of City Hall. As Hoboken's mayor from 1930 to 1947, McFeely led the city through the Great Depression and World War II.

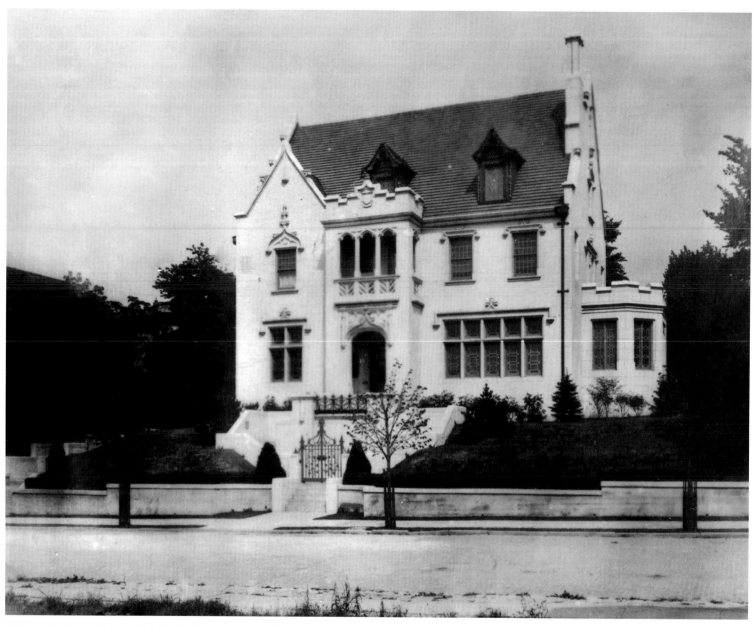

The stately home of Dr. and Mrs. Paul Hoening seen here in 1932 was located at Castle Point in Hoboken.

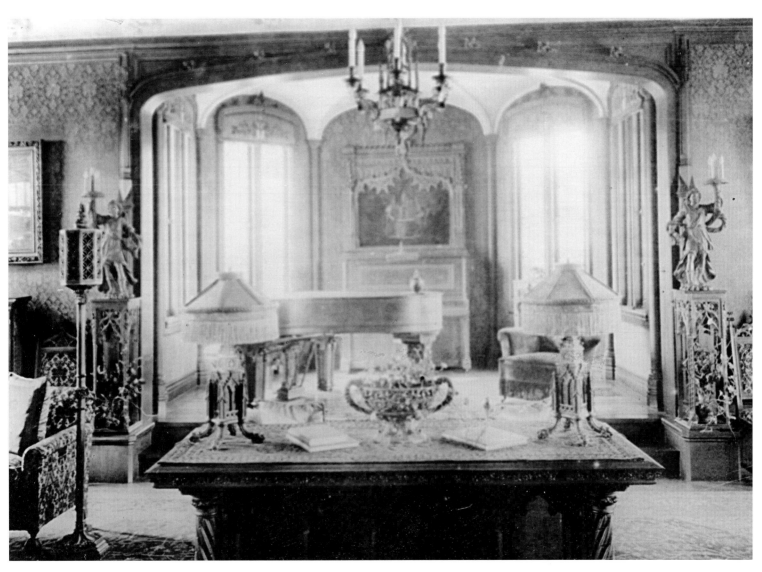

This interior view of the Hoening residence shows a piano and other features of the room's décor.

This 1933 image of the main delivery room of the Hoboken Public Library includes a shell from the USS *Maine* in the foreground.

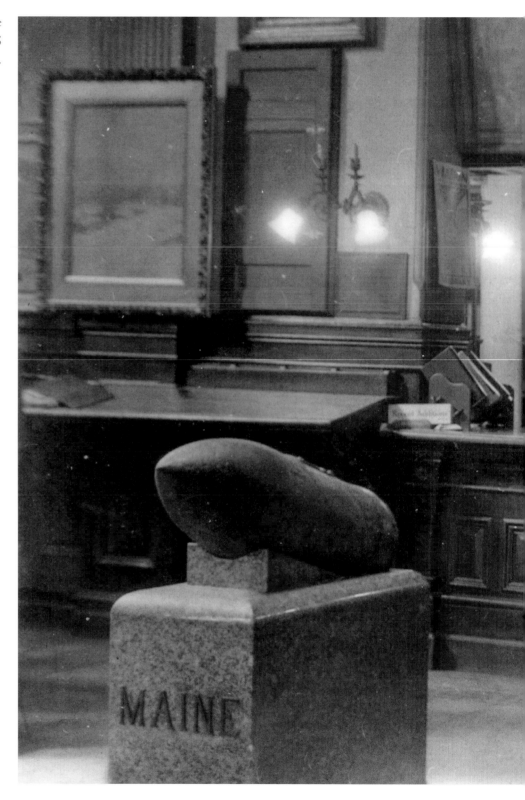

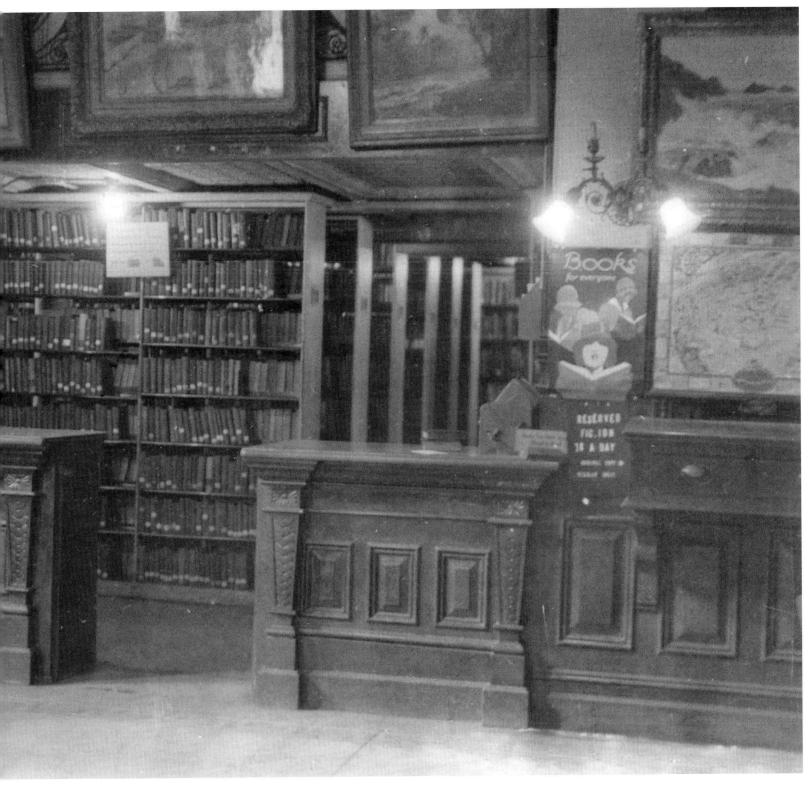

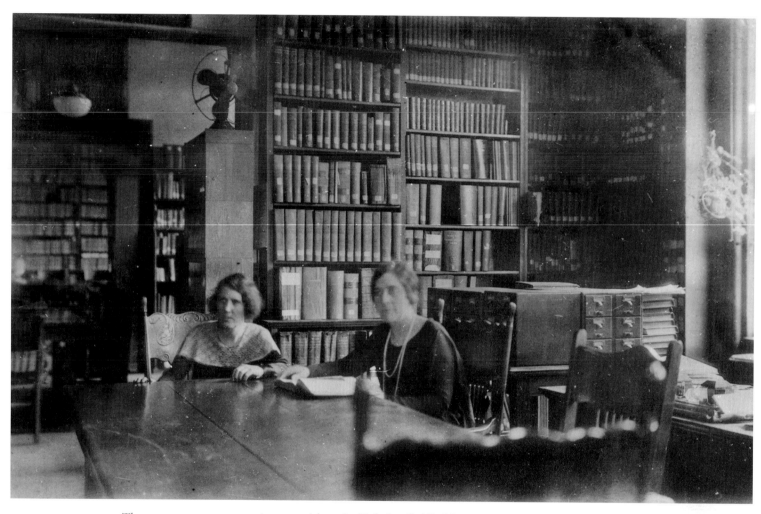

These two women are perusing materials at the Hoboken Public Library in 1933 in what is probably the reference department.

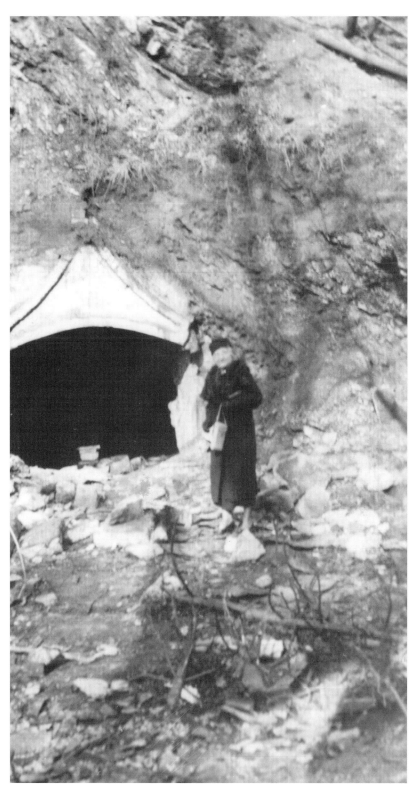

A woman stands outside the entrance of Sybil's Cave in 1937. The cave and the well inside it are said to have been the inspiration for Edgar Allen Poe's story "The Mystery of Marie Roget," his sequel to "The Murders in the Rue Morgue." The cave was at one time operated as a spa advertising artesian waters.

Wooden planks cover the well inside Sybil's Cave near Stevens Institute. The cave opened as a resort in 1832 and was shut in the 1880s due to health concerns, but it remained a major attraction in Hoboken well into the 1930s. It inspired many legends and fables.

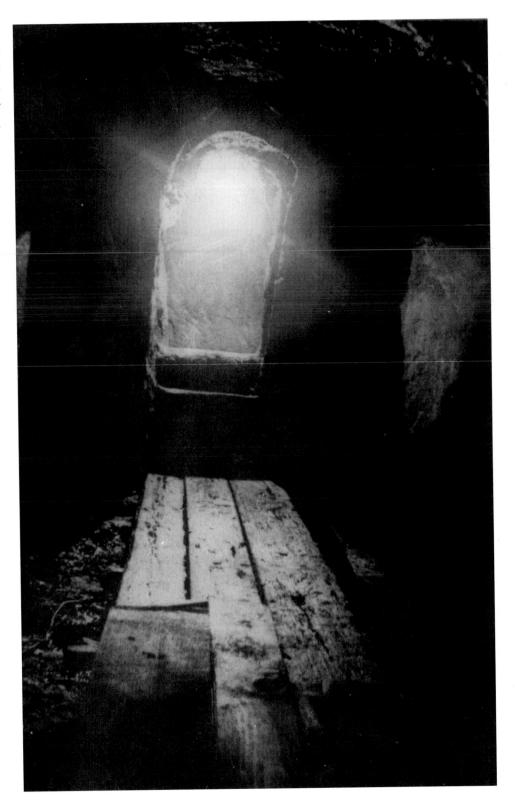

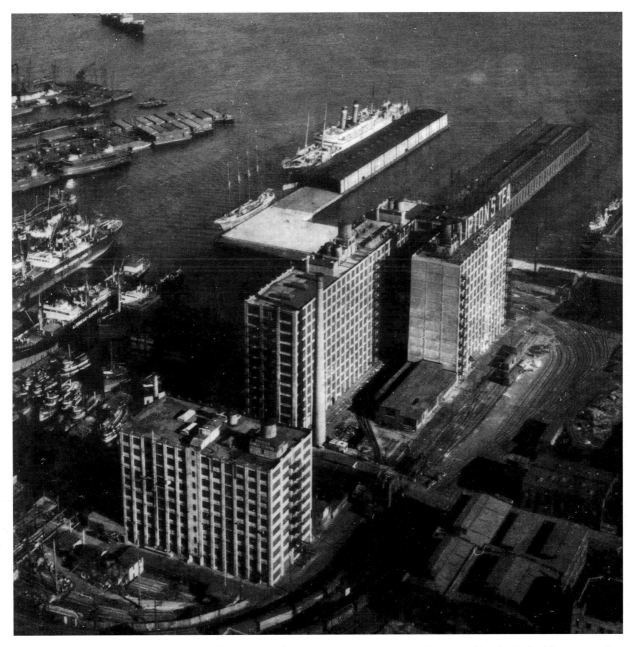

A 1930s aerial view of the uptown waterfront shows the Lipton Tea Company. In the cove, ships loaded with cargoes of tea would anchor and unload directly onto the docks. Sir Thomas Lipton was a member of the Hoboken Chamber of Commerce in 1919.

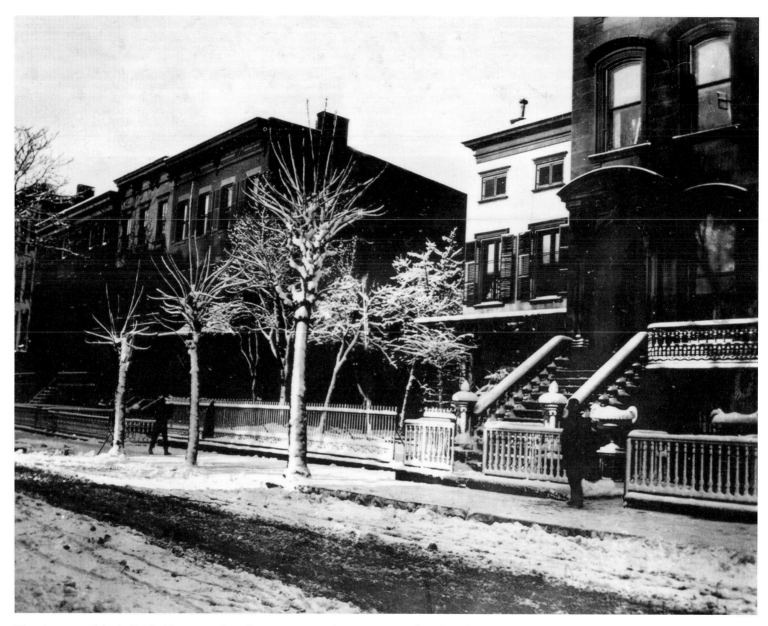

The closeness of the individual homes and small apartments in this 1930s view of Hudson between 2nd and 3rd streets illustrates the tight quarters of the port cities built early on in America. People lived near to where they worked because they traveled on foot to their jobs. Large docks and warehouses employed many people, so neighbors learned one another's habits very well.

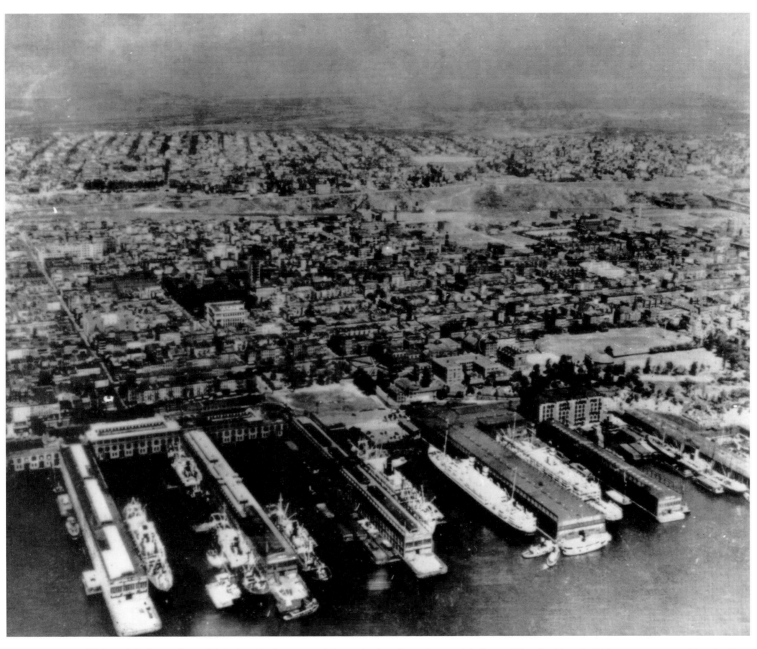

This aerial photo shows Hoboken built outward from the bustling piers at 4th Street. The docking facilities were operated by the Port Authority of New York and New Jersey. Ships, both passenger and cargo, arrived and departed daily; the destination could be anywhere in the world.

The *Leviathan,* aptly named, dwarfs its neighbor ships here in 1932 and barely fits into Pier A. Built in Germany and called the *Vaterland,* it was seized in 1917 and used for transport, ferrying over 120,000 men. After World War I, it was turned over to the United States Shipping Board and was scrapped in 1938. With displacement of 58,000 tons, the *Leviathan* was the largest ship of its day, not surpassed in size until 1945 when the aircraft carrier *Midway* was completed.

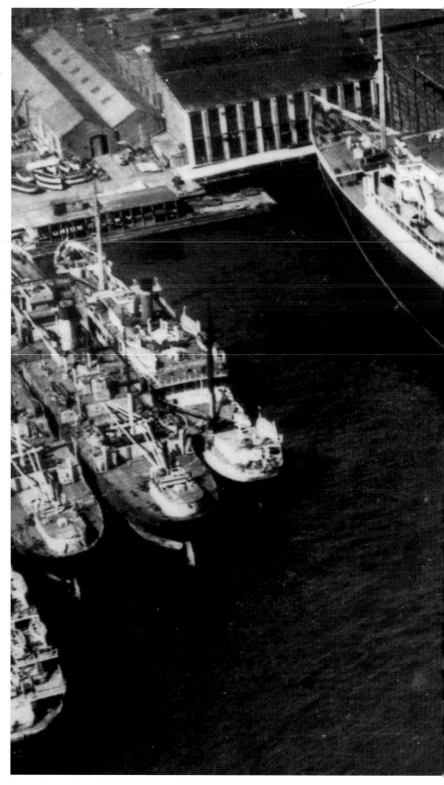

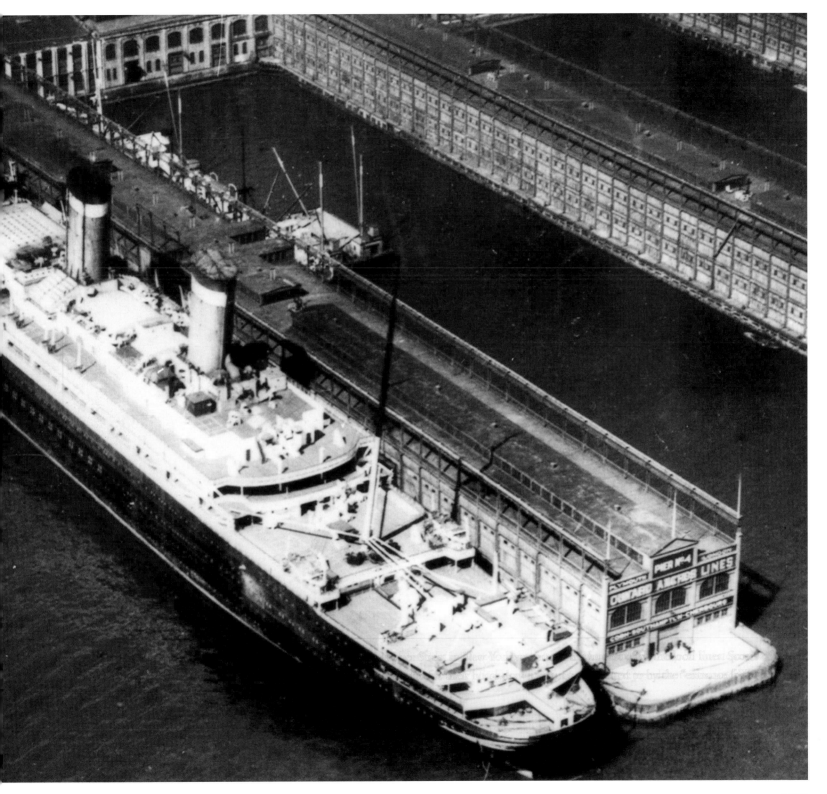

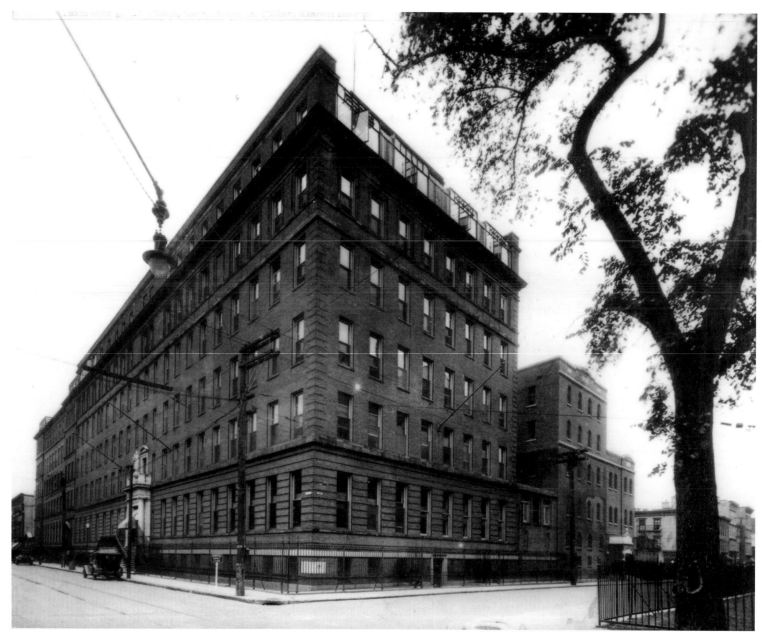

By the 1930s, as seen here, St. Mary's Hospital had reached another stage of development, matching the city's needs.

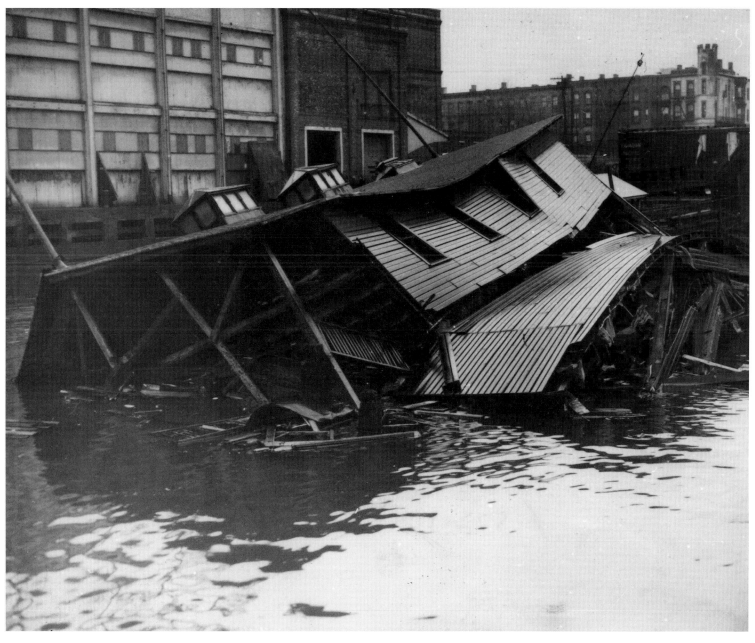

The Atlantic Club boathouse, here collapsed in April 1946, was rebuilt a number of times through the years. Organized in 1858 by the Tuthill Brothers, the Atlantic Club was victorious in numerous rowing races on the Hudson River. By 1893 the club claimed to be the second-oldest rowing association in the United States.

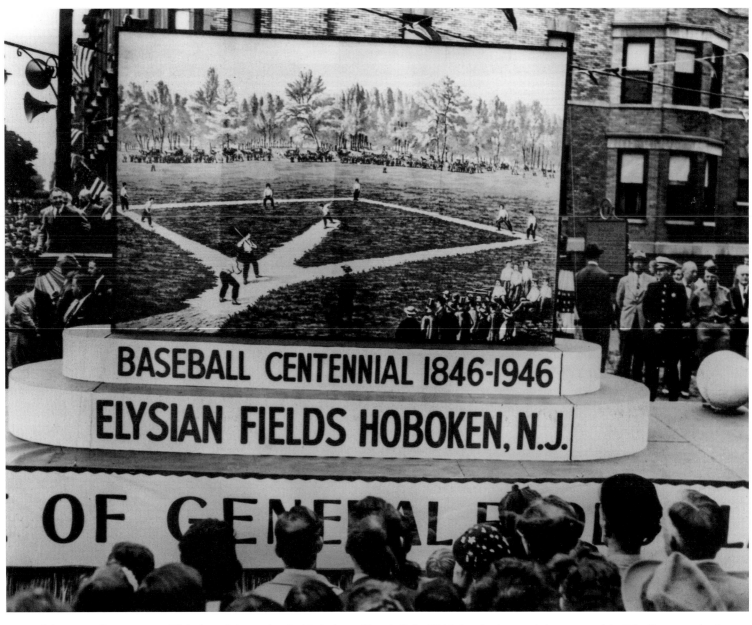

Move over Cooperstown; Hoboken claims to be the birthplace of baseball. In 1946 the city honored the centennial of the first organized game played at the Elysian Fields. This parade float depicts the event.

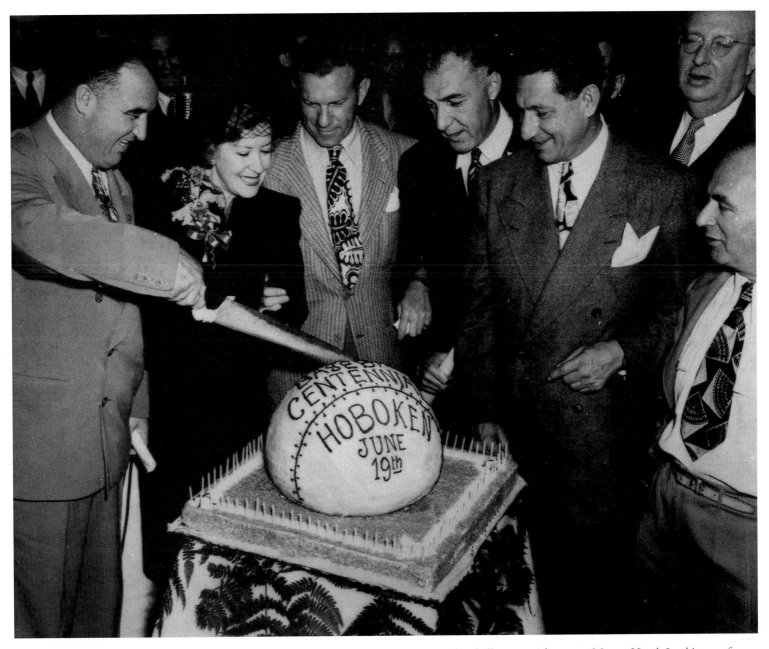

A cake donated by General Foods is cut by baseball commissioner Happy Chandler at a baseball centennial party at Meyers Hotel. Looking on from left to right are Gracie Allen, George Burns, National League commissioner Ford Frick, and the famous "Clown Prince of Baseball," Al Schacht.

Following spread: A dedicated Hoboken fire fighter tends to an engine during a 1945 fire at 1015 Grand Street. Every port city lived in constant fear of fire. Because of dangerous winds coming off the water, a small flame could be blown into frenzy in minutes. Such was the fate of Hoboken many times throughout the years because of wooden ships, wooden structures, sparks from shipping and machinery, and carelessness.

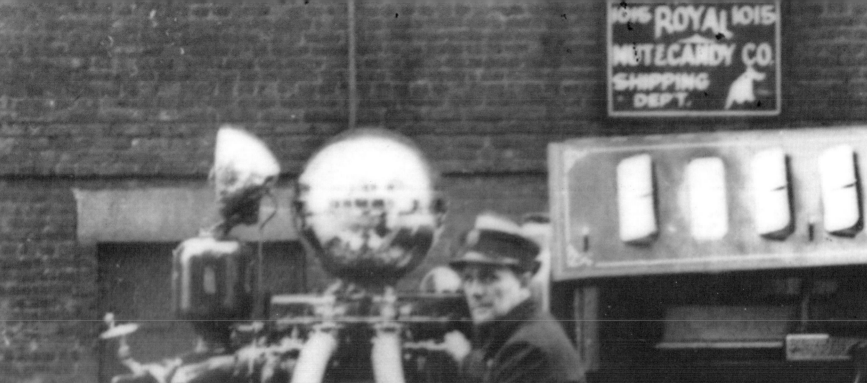
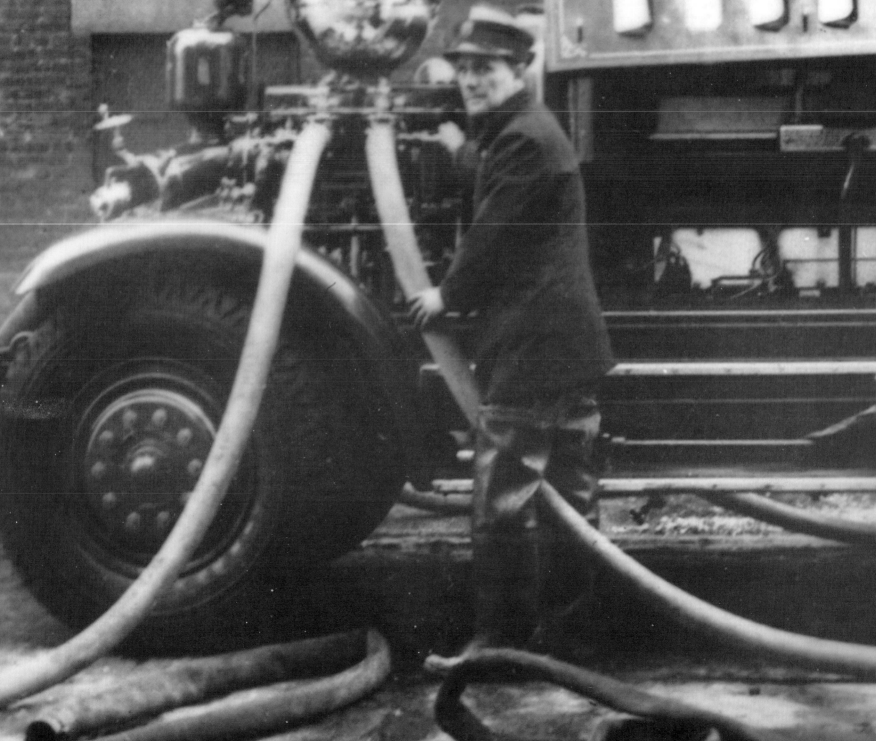

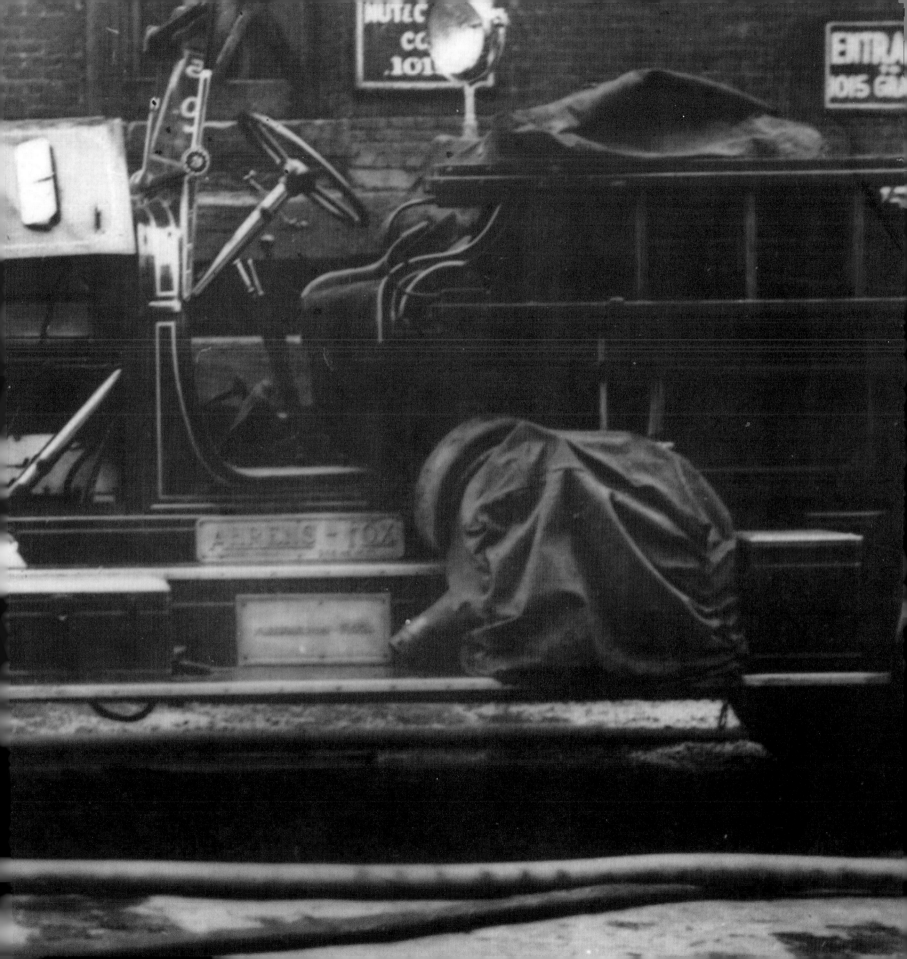

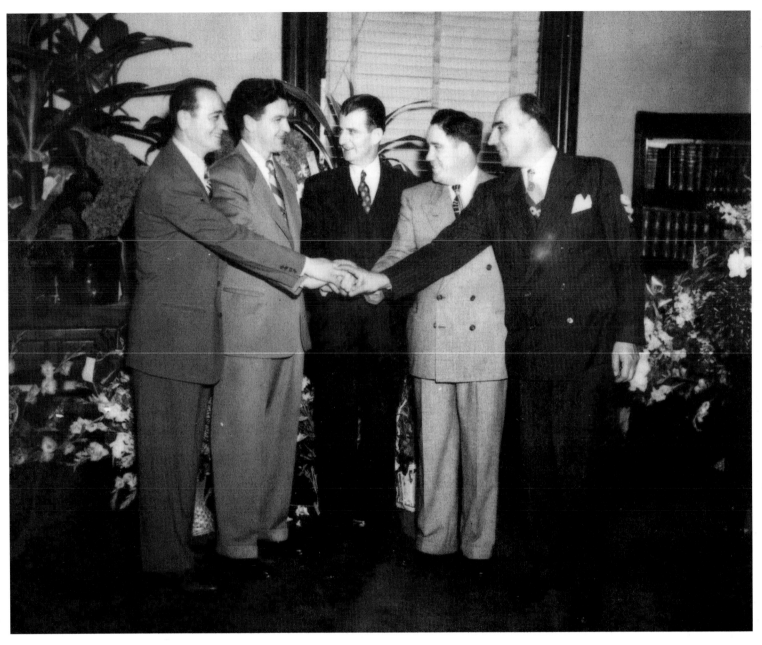

Congratulations all around inside Mayor Fred De Sapio's office in 1947 as the mayor, at left, meets with Hoboken city commissioners Grogan, Borelli, Fitzpatrick, and Mongiello, as seen left to right.

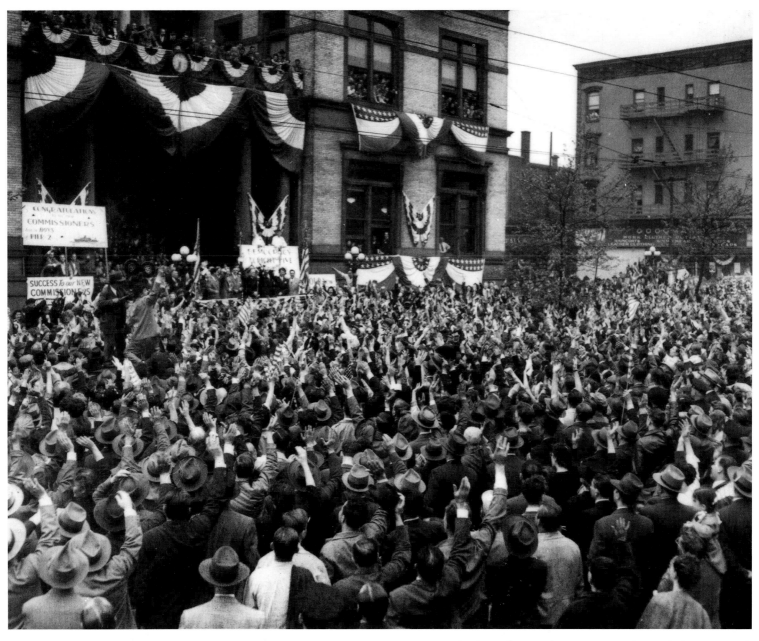

Election Day, May 8th, 1948, drew a large and energetic crowd to Hoboken City Hall.

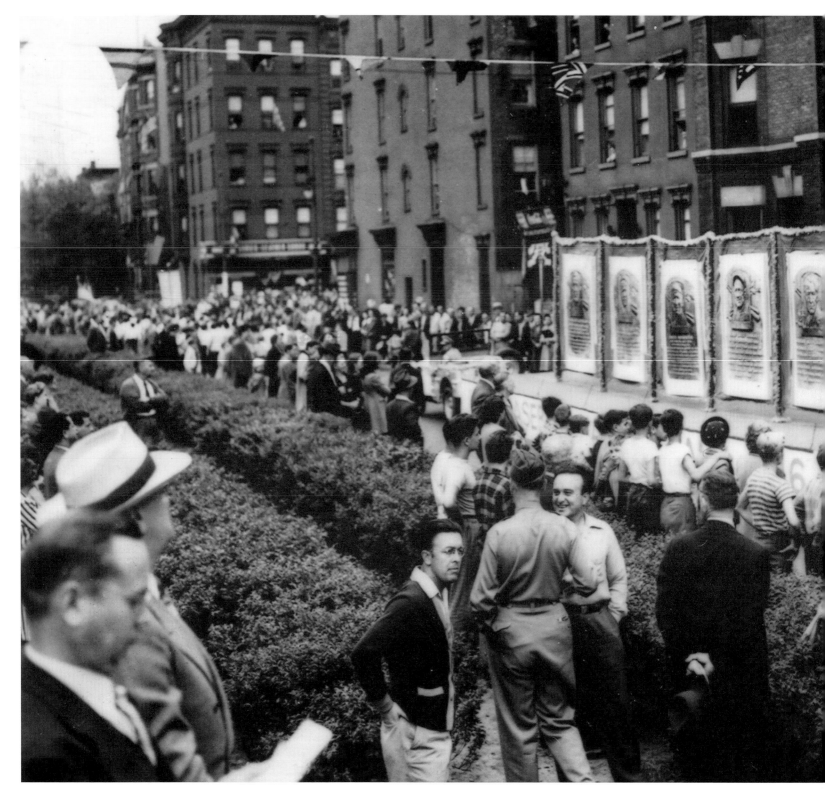

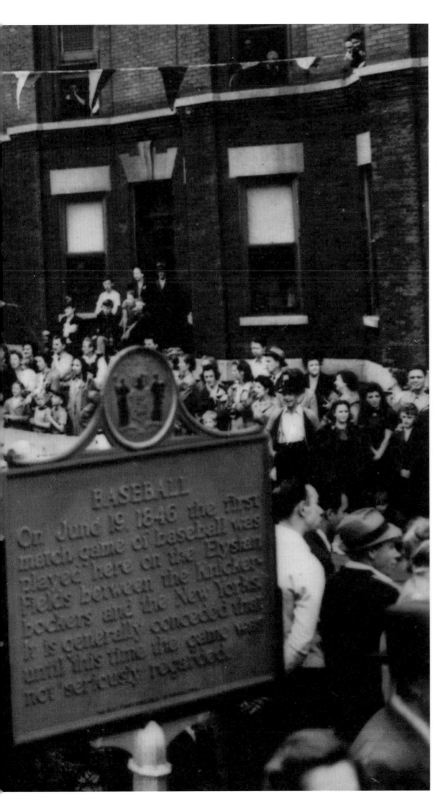

The plaque commemorating "the first match game of baseball" is on Hoboken's 11th Street near Washington Street looking east.

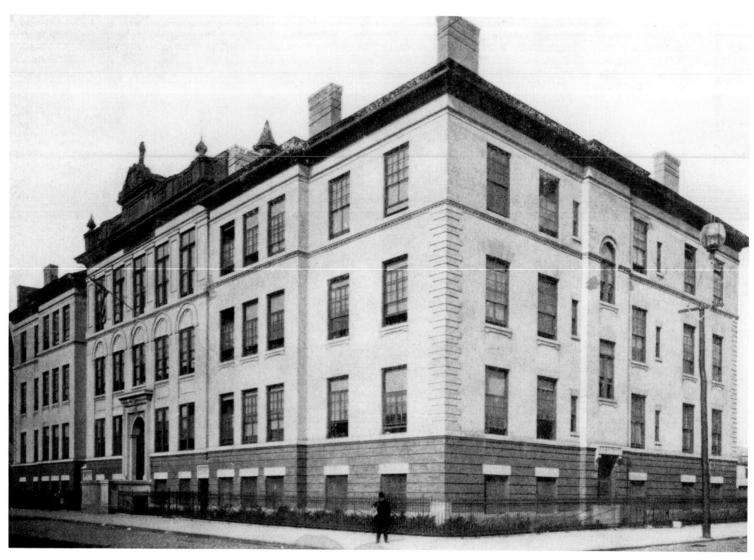

School No. 8, seen here on the corner of 7th and Jefferson streets, was dedicated to the memory of Miss Sadie Leinhauf on October 1, 1947. With Hoboken struggling economically later on, the building would be abandoned in 1980 and converted to condominiums in 1986.

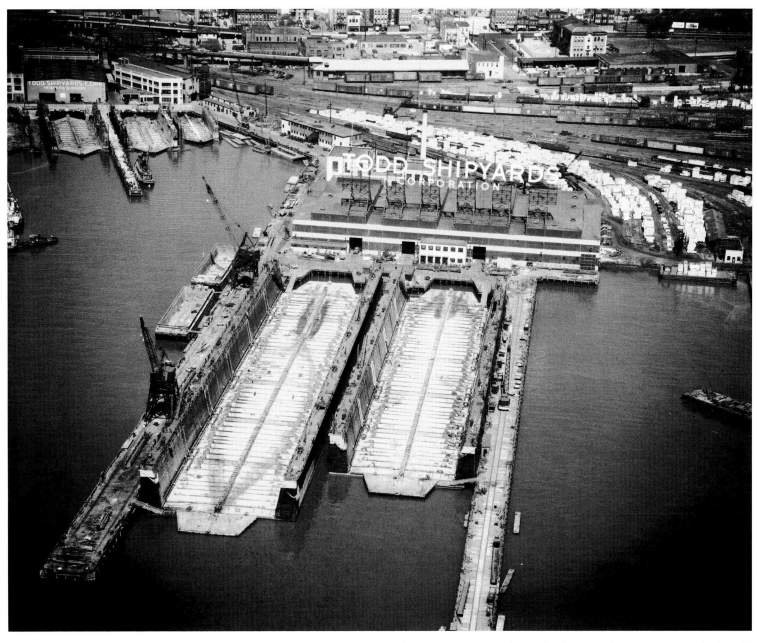

This is a 1951 view of Todd Shipyards on 17th Street, originally the Tietjen and Lang Shipyard, where Frank Sinatra once worked. Todd incorporated several such yards on the East and West coasts and luckily was able to survive the Great Depression. Between December 7, 1941, and August 31, 1945, over 23,000 auxiliary naval ships essential to the war effort were produced by Todd.

During the 1930s in
Hoboken, railroad cars
were loaded on ships
to be transported as far
away as Havana, Cuba.
In 1945 the aptly named
Seatrain line took over
the pier. Business was so
good that the Hoboken
Shore Railroad was later
established for movement
along the waterfront.

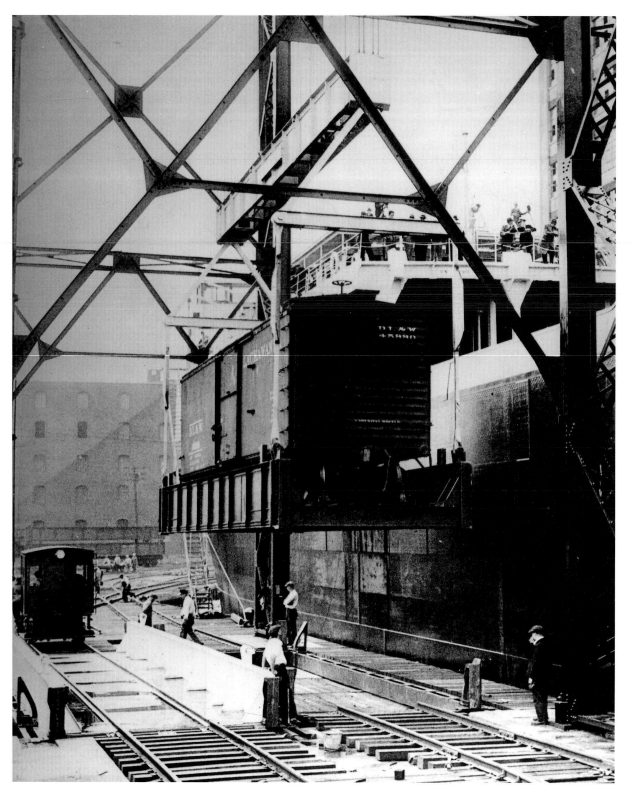

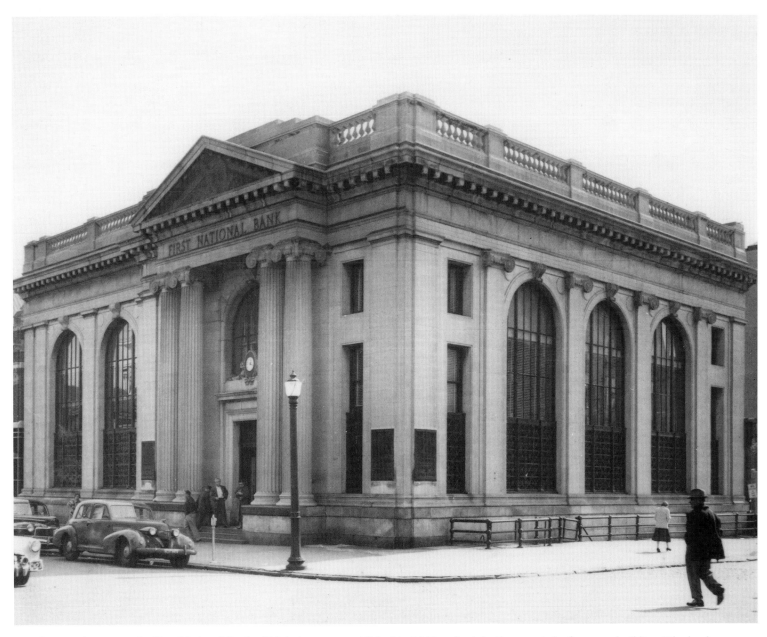

Seen here in the 1950s, the First National Bank of Hoboken was established in 1865 and originally occupied a five-story building. The bank later merged with the Hudson Trust Company; its first executive leader was S. Bayard Dod, a former minister.

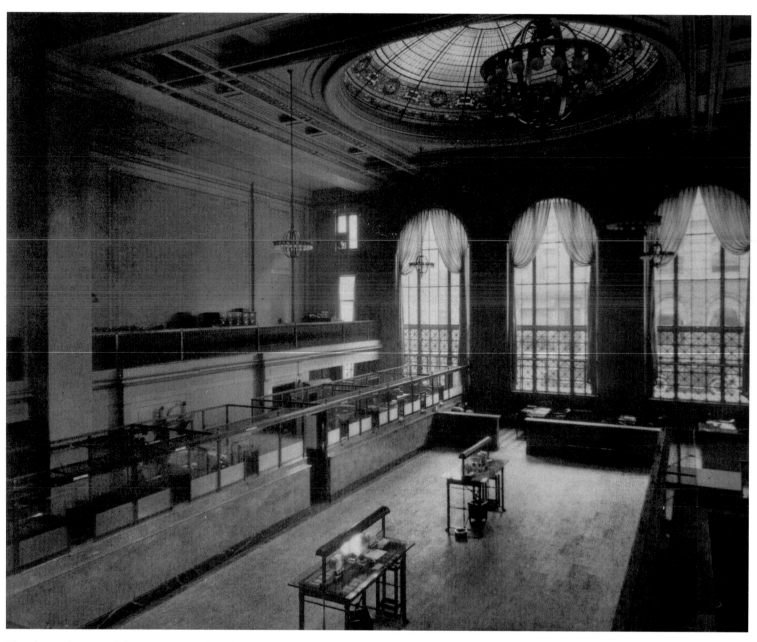

The elegant interior of the First National Bank at Newark and Hudson streets featured an ornate chandelier and a ceiling with a stained-glass dome.

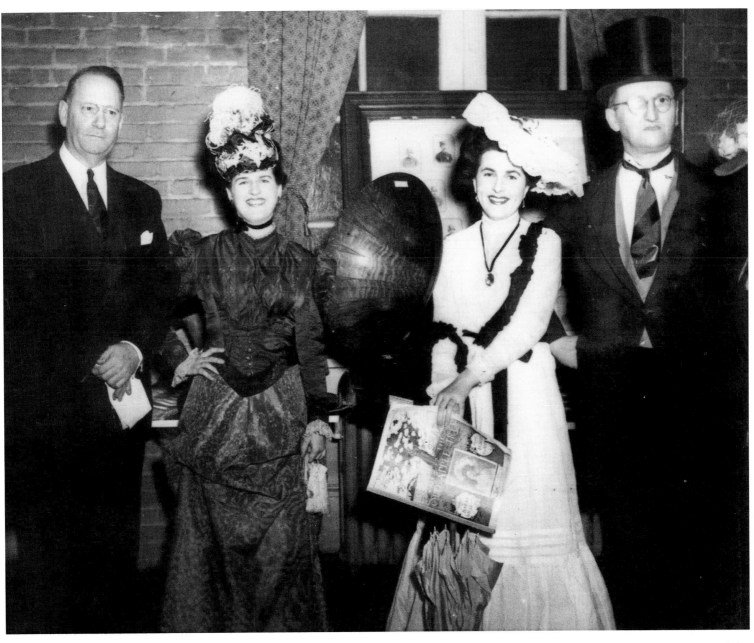

George Miller, Mary and Frances Caughlin, and Adolph Rochich pose at the Waldheim-Stevens Forum during a 1950s celebration. Philip Waldheim was a wealthy leather merchant who in his will bequeathed $75,000 to establish the Public Forum for the Exchange of Ideas in 1921. The site of this soiree was 916 Garden Street, now the site of Hoboken's first automated parking garage.

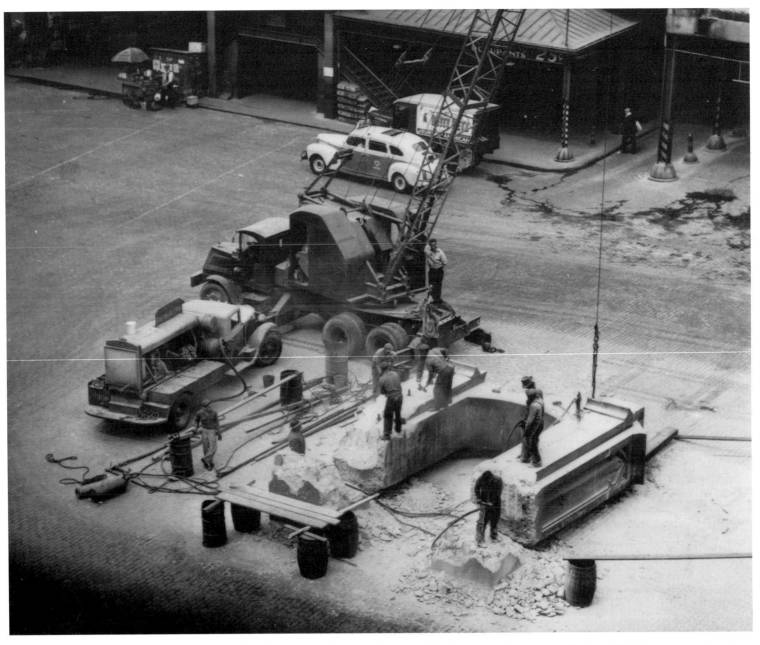

Hoboken ferries ran continuously for 145 years until 1967 and operated the last steam ferry on the Hudson. This Barclay Street location, originally the Hoboken Ferry Company, would be active from half an hour before sunrise until eight or nine at night, depending on the season.

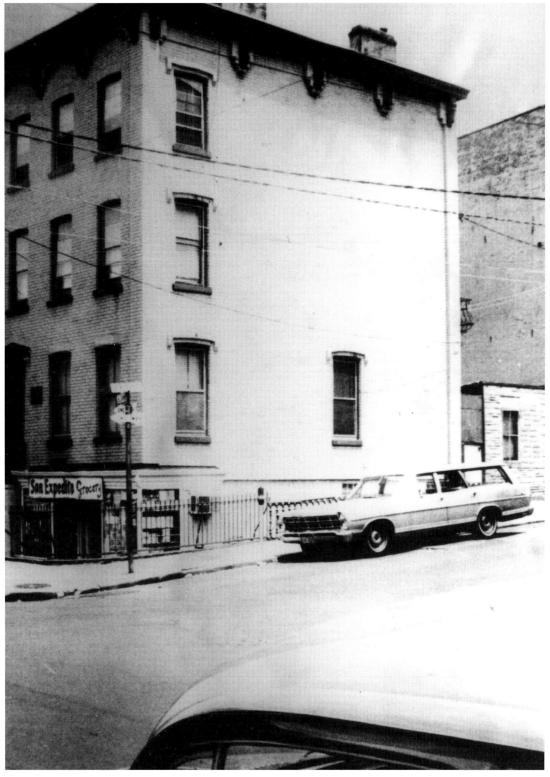

This house at the corner of Bloomfield and 6th streets in the mid-1950s is said to have once been occupied by the legendary songwriter Stephen Foster. He penned "Beautiful Dreamer," "My Old Kentucky Home," "Jeannie with the Light Brown Hair," and "Oh! Susanna," all of which became popular American standards.

The First Presbyterian Church seen here in the 1950s was located at Hudson and 6th streets. Organized in 1852, the church originally was located at Washington and 3rd streets. The first pastor was Issac B. Stryker, and at one point the future banker S. B. Dod was an acting pastor. This building was eventually sold to a German Lutheran congregation and was demolished in 1964 when the congregation moved to the Hoboken Masonic Lodge.

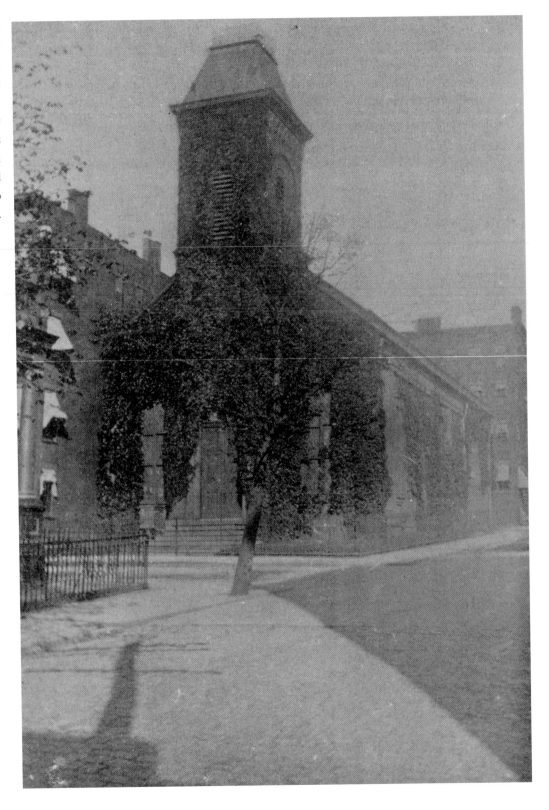

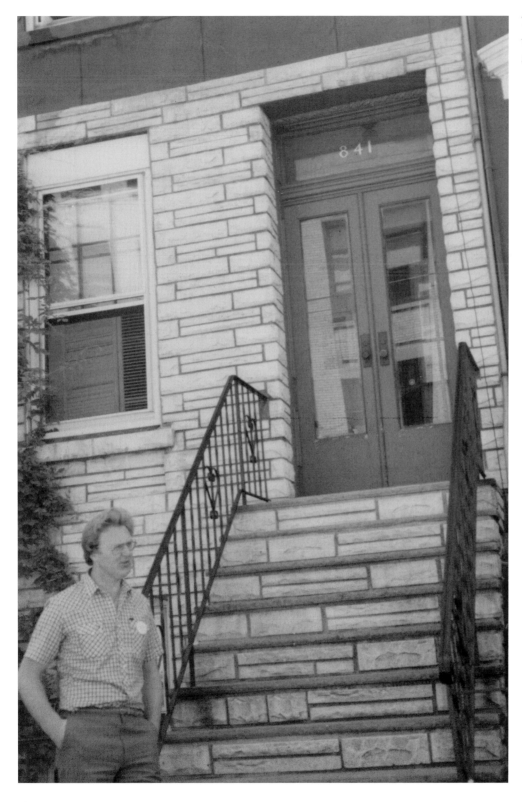

The house at 841 Garden Street in Hoboken was the Sinatra family home when Frank Sinatra was a teen.

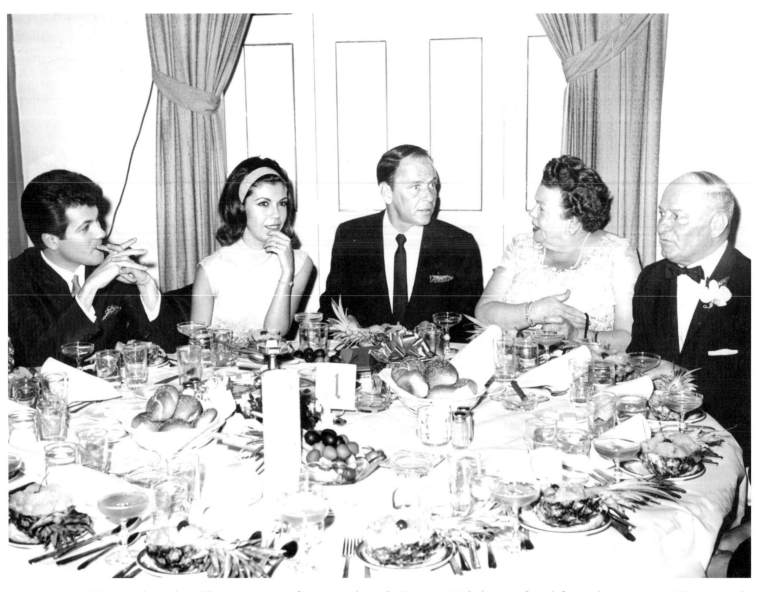

Celebrating the 50th wedding anniversary of Martin and Natalie Sinatra in Hoboken are, from left to right, actor-singer Tommy Sands; Nancy Sinatra, Frank's daughter; Frank; and Natalie and Martin, Frank's parents.

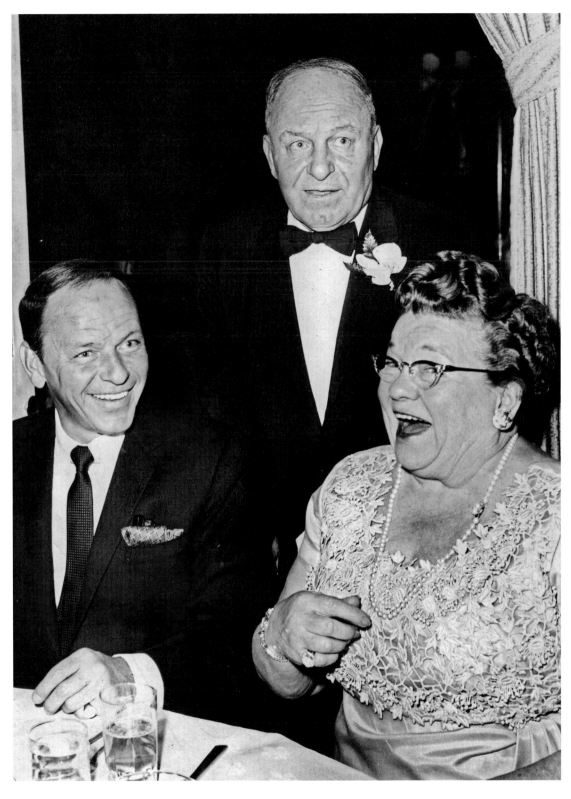

This close-up of the Sinatra family shows quite a resemblance between Frank and his father. Martin Sinatra was a boxer for a short time before operating a tavern called Marty O'Brien's, the name he boxed under. He later became a captain in the Hoboken Fire Department. Natalie Sinatra worked as a barmaid at Marty's and was a Democratic Party ward boss who could guarantee 500 votes on Election Day.

NOTES ON THE PHOTOGRAPHS

These notes, listed by page number, attempt to include all aspects known of the photographs. Each of the photographs is identified by the page number, photograph's title or description, photographer and collection, archive, and call or box number when applicable. Although every attempt was made to collect all available data, in some cases complete data was unavailable due to the age and condition of some of the photographs and records.